"This book is a must for anyone who f
shattered by a loss. Al Johnson not only
walk. You will be inspired by his thoug
take to restore hope and joy in your life."

   —GLORIA HORSLEY and HEIDI HORSLEY, Open to Hope Foundation

"Al Johnson is exactly the kind of caring pastor and wise elder to which any
person in grief would go for comfort. I respect him greatly and am grateful
that he is telling his story of grief and healing."

   —BRIAN D. MCLAREN, author of *Faith after Doubt*

"Al refuses to simply skim the surface of his loss. Instead, . . . he dares to dive
deep into the dark places of his soul, asking the questions with brutal honesty that anyone asks in the face of tragic loss. This book offers tremendous
wisdom not only for those who grieve, but perhaps even more for those of
us who seek to walk with the grieving in loving, more helpful ways."

   —NANCY BEACH, author of *Gifted to Lead:
   The Art of Leading as a Woman in the Church*

"Al Johnson is a rare combination: he loves and listens with calmness and
intention, then leads with action and inspiration, which allows him to be
effective in the numerous ways required of a priest who becomes great, as
he has."

   —BRYAN CRESSEY, President, Cressey Co.

"From time to time, one reads a book that strikes right to the heart of the
human experience of love, death, and hope. This is that book. Written with
elegance and power, Johnson takes us into his life as a father, husband, and
priest who tragically loses his son. The book is beautiful and hopeful."

   —IAN S. MARKHAM, Dean, Virginia Theological Seminary

"Al Johnson's book touched very deep places within me, as it will in you. He
is brave and vulnerable, honest and real in visiting the deep places within
himself where grief still lives and hasn't left—but that grief has finally become the holy mystery of freedom too . . . his own grief set free. . . . Al's

thoughts and words about faith have helped me look even more deeply into my own faith and belief in ways I've needed to do, and his words in this book have given me this holy gift."

—JAN WALKER, author, speaker, priest

"Father Johnson writes for those who are exhausted with the clichés of the grieving journey and yet still hope for time when joy returns after a horrific loss. Only someone who has experienced the abyss of losing a child could write with such honesty, authority, and promise. *Grief Set Free* is the most genuinely Christian book on grief that I've read."

—DAVID GOETZ, author of *Death by Suburb*

"Al Johnson allows us to travel with him down the path of anger, despair, and heartbreak toward a profound understanding of God's love and compassion. Through Al's heartfelt story, we come to understand grief as an agent of growth and discovery, and our church congregations as communities where we can offer God's healing mercy to one another. Bereaved parents and those who seek to comfort them will finish this poignant book knowing they are not alone."

—SEAN ROWE, Episcopal Bishop of Northwestern Pennsylvania

Grief Set Free

Grief Set Free

A Memoir

ALVIN JOHNSON

CASCADE *Books* · Eugene, Oregon

GRIEF SET FREE
A Memoir

Cascade Books
An Imprint of Wipf and Stock Publishers
199 W. 8th Ave., Suite 3
Eugene, OR 97401

www.wipfandstock.com

PAPERBACK ISBN: 978-1-7252-9399-1
HARDCOVER ISBN: 978-1-7252-9398-4
EBOOK ISBN: 978-1-7252-9400-4

Cataloguing-in-Publication data:

Names: Johnson, Alvin C., author. Myers, Robert K., Jr., foreword.

Title: Grief set free : a memoir / Alvin C. Johnson.

Description: Eugene, OR: Cascade Books, 2022 | Includes bibliographical references.

Identifiers: ISBN 978-1-7252-9399-1 (paperback) | ISBN 978-1-7252-9398-4 (hardcover) | ISBN 978-1-7252-9400-4 (ebook)

Subjects: LCSH: Children—Death—Psychological aspects. | Bereavement—Psychological aspects. | Fathers and sons.

Classification: BF575.G7 .J50 2022 (print) | BF575.G7 (ebook)

The select portion of the poem "Kindness" is used by permission of the author, Naomi Shihab Nye, from *Everything Comes Next & New Poems*, Greenwillow Books, 2020.

Scripture quotations are from the New Revised Standard Version Bible, copyright © 1989 National Council of the Churches of Christ in the United States of America. Used by permission. All rights reserved worldwide.

The names of the actual persons mentioned, with a few exceptions because the author cannot connect with the family due to death, are the persons' actual names. Each is used with permission.

This book is dedicated to my wife, Vickie,
and to Hannah, Zachary,
and, of course, to Nicholas.

"Hear, O Lord, and have mercy upon me

O Lord, be my helper."

You have turned my wailing into dancing;

You put off my sackcloth and clothed me with joy.

Therefore, my heart sings to you without ceasing;

O Lord, my God, I will give you thanks forever.[1]

---

1. *Book of Common Prayer*, 622.

Table of Contents

Foreword

OUR SON, ANDREW JOHN Myers, was born three months premature and weighed slightly over one pound. He spent nearly three months in the neonatal unit of the hospital, clinging to life. He had surgery to repair a patent ductus, and he arrested once. Subsequently, we learned he was developmentally disabled, profoundly deaf, and had mild cerebral palsy. During the early years of his life, he was compulsive about opening and closing doors, a ritual he would perform repeatedly until he was redirected. Redirecting lasted only for a short time, and then he was back to the doors. Opening and closing. Moving from one side to the other. Examining. Front doors, back doors, bedroom doors, closet doors, any door—it didn't matter. He worked on doors. Hinges would come loose. Handles wiggled. What was this about?

I spoke with the psychiatric consultant of the pastoral counseling center where I worked. Mary was also the consultant to the neonatal unit where Andrew was born. She shared her perspective. Andrew spent his early months clinging to life. Each day, the door of his small isolette was opened and closed many hundreds of times as nurses monitored him, changed him, fed him, provided medications, among other duties. What would it be like for any of us, regardless of age—immobilized, fragile, teetering between life and death, and someone comes in and out of your space hundreds of times a day? Imagine what a tiny neonatal baby experienced. She believed Andrew was working some of that precognitive experience out. Who is on the other side of that door as it opens? What do they want? Will they hurt me? What is the world they are in? What is it like 'out there'? Who is entering my space? Andrew spent years in his door of exploration.

Isn't this the way of us all? From birth to death, the maturational process is one of discovery. What is life "out there"? Most of us spend our lives seeking answers. Incidentally, the isolette could be opened from the outside, but not the inside. We wait for someone to open the door.

Father Al opens the door of his soul and invites us in. We can't open that door. There are no handles on our side. Only he can open the door for us and invite us to be with him. We are humbled to witness what "this beautiful boy's death" has done to him, his beloved wife, Vickie, the children, and their respective extended families. Their journey takes them into the lives of others who have lost a child. Their story is long and unending, yet it brings insights along the way. Grief is an enduring struggle. It poses questions: What meaning can there be? How does one cope? Is there ever peace? Does grief end? Will we meet again? What would it be like were I to experience the same? There are no pat answers or simple formulas through this doorway. Al challenges easy and quick solutions. Grief is not resolved with stages or ordered steps. It lingers. Here is a human soul revealing his multifaceted, deeply gripping experience. Thank you, sir, for your courage and determination in bringing us this memoir.

Al experiences Nicholas's death as passing through a doorway. He desperately wants to go back through that doorway to the life before this death. His attempts are for naught. There is no handle on that side of the door to be opened so relief can be found. There is no turning back. Death is cruel and does not allow such things. "Pounding on the door, hoping someone would hear and open it," doesn't repay the effort. The totality and finality of death are absolute. This reading is not for the faint of heart, though there is humor to be found as well. Al shares his vulnerability and questioning. His life as a priest does not provide him the sanctuary of a safe, prescribed place. He struggles. The symbol of our faith is a cross, a bewildering symbol of fear, abuse of power, loneliness, sorrow, ache, and death. Glory is found finally, only in the suffering. Because of Al's openness, we are observers/participants of the inner world of loss. Along the way we meet his family, other parents of loss, friends, companions, rituals, an old orange chair, and the importance of Reese's Cups, among other things.

He is fatigued and alone waiting at the door. His crying out offers no resolve. And so, he decides to get up and move. In doing so, he finds that he is not alone and that there are other doors, other aching souls. He finds that Vickie is there too. Doors become visible everywhere. The others are fatigued and fearful of loneliness as well. Brother Martin Smith reminds Al that he is forever connected to all those parents who grieve and those yet to come. It is a fraternity of those who grieve the loss of a child. They have a committed doorkeeper. He doesn't seek handles. There are none. He seeks companions who love. He embodies wisdom, the wisdom of a faithful, aching heart. Like Humpty Dumpty, the shattered heart is not reassembled. Putting everything back together again isn't the goal.

One day, an heroic nurse opened Andrew's isolette from the outside for the last time. He came home. Father Al has opened a door and invited us to be free. What we find is an eagle flying in the storm. Because he is valiant, he struggles through the drenching rains, soaring above the clouds and reaching the sunlight. Thank you, Al, for being an eagle. Thank you for soaring and sharing the light you have found: *Grief Set Free*.

The Reverend Robert K. Myers, Jr., PhD

Preface

LIFE IS SHORT, SHORTER for some than for others. Our son Nicholas died at age seven from leukemia in 1989, now more than thirty years ago. I've tried to write this book before, but the timing just wasn't right. A memoir about death of children takes time to season. Some books can only be written in the second half of life when life's experiences are to be plumbed; this is one of them. Earlier versions of this idea were too angry, too prescriptive, or too sorrowful. Earlier versions would have invited the reader to resolve, get over, or move beyond their loss. Earlier versions would have exhorted the reader to find happiness somewhere viewing grief and joy as an oxymoron versus the good friends they really are. They do, after all, coexist in all our experiences of death and life.

This is a book about setting grief free so we may experience grief in a way that takes into account our uniqueness as individuals. Setting grief free allows grief to run its natural course as our lives move to enfold all the experiences of suffering that form and condition our souls. Set free, grief becomes only one of many emotions that affect and drive our lives, and it gives us a perspective by which we remember our dead loved ones, drawn powerfully into our present times. Our culture thinks grief is a battle to win. In reality grief is a critical experience of life that forms us deep in our souls and in our spiritual selves. Grief set free leads us to see suffering as an integral and nonnegotiable reality of our lives, allowing us to feel what we feel and to bring healing and wholeness as we draw our lives together with "those we love but see no longer."

For many, the idea of setting grief free may seem quite improbable. We labor to "get over" our losses. We hold the truth of our experience privately and cry alone in the car, and we wonder if there is something wrong with us because we still get sad. Our secrets become different as they focus on our memory and our silent struggle to move on in our lives. Expectations of grief seem so readily prescribed by others who have never lived one moment of our lives, from our truth and from our perspective. Is it possible that, in setting grief free, we might, ourselves, be set free? I like to think so.

Ultimately, you will decide whether this book calls you to a different way of living. It is both my hope and my prayer that we step away from the boredom, fear, and pressure of grieving to a place of grief set free where we can bring into our lives, for all our lives, the losses and the joys that mark and define our souls. Your story is unique. It's the story that got you on this path in the first place, and it's the story that eventually will lead you to appreciate the path your life now takes, along with the richness that accompanies you on your way. This book is by no means an attempt to lessen or diminish the intensity of the losses of our lives. But now, over thirty years after our son Nicholas's death, I have come to realize that loved ones live on in the stories of our lives.

Acknowledgments

Thanks to Vickie, my lifelong partner whose love and support enabled this memoir to be born. I thank her, too, for the joy of being her husband.

Thanks to Hannah and Zachary for their unfailing and unconditional love and for the exquisite joy of being their father. And for Katy and Ben.

Thanks to Kitten Penney for her incredible editorial assistance through two different versions of this work. She introduced me to the grace of commas.

Thanks to Mary Kay Shanley and Jennifer Fawcett from the Iowa Writers' Workshop.

Thanks to Rodney Clapp, Cascade Books editor, for his help in making this a better offering, and to Cascade in general for the grace of publishing this story.

Thanks to Dave Goetz, who years ago, with *Leadership* magazine, challenged me to tell this story and then, later, was honest with his ideas.

Thanks to the early readers: Bob Myers, Paul Johnson, Vickie Johnson, Hannah Johnson, Zachary Johnson, Jan Walker, Ian Markham, Sean Rowe, Brian McLaren, Kay Phillips, and Dave Goetz.

Thanks to my dear friend, Bob Myers.

Thanks to Bill and Jane Kindorf, Fr. Michael Sparough, and to Jim Gruenwald.

ACKNOWLEDGMENTS

Thanks to the many souls mentioned, all by name, throughout the memoir, for their willingness to offer bits of their lives for healing and for storytelling.

Thanks to my parents, Vickie's parents and brother, and my three wonderful siblings and their circles of family.

And thank you to Nicholas for the example of his life, for his courage in the face of illness and death, and for the exquisite joy of being his father.

Introduction

I BEGAN SERIOUSLY WRITING this memoir in June 2018 for one reason: For the previous two months I had three separate dreams of my dear son Nicholas. I haven't dreamt of him for years. In each of the dreams he appears as the young boy he was when he died. He also appears as he looked battling leukemia, with his bald head and puffed-up cheeks. In every dream he is doing well and in each dream I think he was going to make it through and live, even though I knew he was dead. My heart was strangely warmed. In one case a doctor even appeared and let me know that Nicholas wasn't going to live forever but he was alive and well now. Each time I awoke to a feeling of contentment and curiosity. In my imagination, I asked Nicholas what he wanted to say to me. He wanted me to know he was okay and also wanted me to know it was time to tell the story. He told me in so many words that he was with me and would help me draw myself to acceptance. He told me to embrace love and grief. He forgave me.

I don't know how you feel about mystical experiences. Some say dreams are God's forgotten language; or, in my case, a sense of my son's presence in my own spirit and soul; or glimpses of heaven. It doesn't matter. It's the message and the messenger together that compel me to write a memoir on grief. Why has it taken so long to write? Sometimes it takes awhile to come to a place where the story can be told as an invitation and healing versus proof or defense. I think this book most of the time comes from that place. Sometimes one must come to a place of gratitude as well and have acceptance of life's mysteries and love, and write from what I'd call a place of redemption. And finally, I was sitting with a friend recently having coffee when she recounted for me the story of her brother drowning when she was eleven. In an offhand comment she noted that it took thirty years for her to begin to process and grieve his death, and I was reminded again that grief set free is grief free to be lived as the grieving person so desires and experiences. And, like our personal theologies, we all have stories of grief and they are all true.

This book has become a memoir because a memoir invites you, the reader, to give and receive as the story unfolds. This is also a memoir because real life always seems more powerful than explanation, theoretical concepts, and "shoulds." This is also a memoir in that every time I tell this painful story my own spirit heals just a bit more; in the telling is the healing. Thank you for reading this.

When two people make love and a child is conceived and born, and/or when we are called to adopt, we envision a life for our child. We think of positive outcomes. Sometimes, honestly, we get too far down the road. Sometimes we forget that the child isn't a trophy for us but a human being that will have his or her own way in spite of our best efforts, coaxing, or demands. Over time we begin to envision a good life for them and, as we get to know them and let them go, we begin to enjoy what they hope their lives will become. Eventually we release them from our expectations and from being responsible for our happiness in any way. We rejoice that they have become adults, selves, and people.

At the same time, we don't sit and imagine all the painful paths our children could follow, or the randomness of tragedy, or the fact of suffering. Nor do we think of what all this might mean to us as parents. My dear departed mother-in-law Tix Arnold use to say, "If you think raising children gets easier as they get older, you've got another thing coming." Back when our first child was very young, I thought Tix didn't know what she was talking about. Looking back now on thirty-nine years of being a dad and seeing the path we have traveled, Tix has become wiser and gets quoted more and more.

Whenever Tix would say this, I could tell she was speaking about pain. When our first child was young my sense of pain was the sacrifice of not having as much freedom as before he was born. I was selfish. She was trying to prepare me for the suffering yet to come, a suffering born of a love so deep that the love cannot be matched by marriage and maybe, maybe, only eclipsed by God's love for all of us. Tix suffered through her son's three failed marriages, his unwillingness to have children, and the alcoholism that would take his life two years after her own death. She died with a broken heart. When she said what she said about older children, Tix was pouring out her own grief in hopes that somehow her experience would anesthetize us. She spoke the truth wrapped ever so generously in unconditional love.

This is a book about love and grief. This book is about sorrow/suffering and joy, about hope and despair. Not as some overly simplistic dualistic philosophical conception of life, but as part of the interesting experiential mix of human experience.

All human relationships end, and relationships of love always end with a mixture of love, sadness, and pain because that to which we are attached in this life, which we feed and feeds us, when taken away, leaves us much less than we were before and yet not still what we can become. And yet who would not give all for love, even though with so much pain? And who would not even give ever so much more for children? Not all of us for sure, but most of us definitely.

When Vickie and I conceived children on three occasions, we had little idea of what would be born of our love. We had no idea that our hearts could be stretched as wide open as they were on August 1, 1981 (Nicholas), on August 4, 1986 (Hannah), and on January 29, 1991 (Zachary). We also had no idea how broken our hearts could become simply by the willingness to love. Hearts crushed, really, by love and healed by that same love. This book is about that love and how love is set free when grief is set free.

Henri Nouwen captures this best: "Do not hesitate to love and to love deeply. You might be afraid of the pain that deep love can cause. When those you love deeply reject you, leave you, or die, your heart will be broken. But that should not hold you back from loving deeply. The pain that comes from deep love makes your love ever more fruitful."[1]

---

1. Nouwen, *Inner Voice*, 59.

Chapter 1

The Door

Before you know kindness as the deepest thing inside
You must know sorrow as the other deepest thing.
You must wake up with sorrow.
You must speak to it till your voice
Catches the thread of all sorrows
And you see the size of the cloth.[1]

THE BEAUTIFUL BOY'S DEATH that is the focus of this memoir threw me painfully through a metaphorical doorway. Had I even seen his death coming and been able to put out my hands and feet to try to stop the process of life from moving forward, I would quickly have learned that's not possible. Death cast me through a doorway and once I landed and realized the strangeness of the new territory, my first inclination was to get up, turn around, and run back through that doorway to whatever was before. Who could blame me? The waves of pain were overwhelming, and I naturally wanted to see if I could return to the prior state.

When I turned around, however, I saw that there was a door, and it was shut. Instinctively I looked for the handle, first on one side then the other. Then frantically I scoured the entire door face only to discover there was no handle. Panic took hold. The old adage that this must be a dream and shortly I'll wake up played in my mind as well.

Not to be dismayed, I began to pick around the edges of the door in hopes of finding a spot to leverage an opening, then I could put in a hand, then a foot, then my entire body and back I'd go to simpler, pain-free times. My hands became bloodied and bruised by my impassioned desire to get

1. Nye, *Everything*, 222.

a hold on the door and open the door to the past. I pounded the door in hopes that someone on the other side would hear me and open up. I pounded and clawed and pounded and clawed and shouted until I became hoarse, and my fingers bloodied, and I collapsed in an exhausted heap at the bottom of the door. And I rested.

When I awakened, I looked one more time to see if there was a way to open the door and return to the past. I was more thoughtful this time and less willing to damage my hands and fingers in hopes that they will begin to heal. I tap, knock, squeeze, and pry the door, all with no luck. Frustration mounts again and, sure enough, this day also ends with me in a heap sitting outside the door, enveloped in tears of sadness and grief, and blinded to the horizon.

How long I stayed by that metaphorical door is unknown. Time seemed to stand still. I might even have gone through the normal activities of my day in work, family, or even play, but then I would return to my place outside the door and await some direction on what was next. And then the truth: no matter what, I will never go back through that door to the life I had before, nor with the people with whom I was living. I collapsed again and again against the door, exhausted from trying to figure out where I was and how to move forward.

One day, however, I finally raised my head and looked around. "I can't sit here forever!" I got up and looked around. There was vegetation and life in many forms, and although I resented that life, still I hungered to be alive, whole and well . . . I wanted to be restored to wholeness, from deep down inside to the very facial expressions I wore. I began to walk forward into an unknown future.

Eventually I saw, to my right and to my left, other people who were also walking. They looked equally sad and burdened. Their eyes were set forward and they seemed to be unaware of what was on either side of them. They walked like the walking dead, but I took hope from the fact they were walking forward. I was convinced that everyone wanted to be alone right now and maybe so. Along the way there were some who were not walking and appeared to be dead. I, however, kept walking and began to see ahead another person nearly on my same path. In a moment there she was, and I engaged. Introductions were forced, yet I felt a strange kinship with this person, as if she understands me and somehow knows my experience. I was met with a warm, sympathetic, and understanding response. My guard dropped, my breath slowed, and my body relaxed.

Perhaps this person knew the key to reopening the door and return-ing. She said, "Did you lose a child?" I replied, "Yes, how did you know?" She took up the growing conversational thread: "That's the path we are on. When we come through the door, we don't notice that there are doors all around us. We're so focused on seeing if we can return through our own door that we convince ourselves we are alone. Just has to be. We must try and try and try on our own, with laser focus, before our vision changes and we begin to look around. I bet what you did was begin walking forward be-cause there was no hope backwards, probably in hopes of finding someone who could open that door? That won't happen. We need each other, and my role in your walk is to reinforce what you already know, that there is no way back through that door to a life that you had before. None. Your life is now going in a different direction that you didn't choose, and you don't want, but here you are."

"Let's see your hands," she said. "Yep, nice job trying to open the door again. Crazy, isn't it? I also lost a child about a month before you did. If you look up there about 100 yards, you'll see another person. That was my real-ity check and my first encounter with a bereaved parent. While the news wasn't good, the hope was knowing that we're not alone in this journey out of the valley. Come along with me now. I'd like to hear your story and I'd like for you to listen to mine." As we walked, we talked, and I listened.

Each time I share the story of loss the burden is lightened and each time I listen to another's story, theirs is lightened as well … just ever so slightly. And our step becomes brisker. Soon we parted but agreed to see each other again and to find a way to stay in touch, this initial community of the brokenhearted.

Soon, as I walked this spiritual and metaphorical path, other people came into view, walking in twos and threes, and yes, there were also other doorways. I wanted desperately to shift over to those paths and save those people the angst of pounding and clawing at the door, but that's not an op-tion. You can't get here without being there and alone. We looked for hope; we become hope by the way we live our lives.

Then one day I passed a group of people on the same path who were talking, and all of a sudden one began to laugh, a deep and resounding, soul-releasing laugh. I was startled: how does one laugh again after so great a sorrow? I became rabidly curious because I was catching glimpses of the possibility for a healed life that was invisible to me years ago, but now began to show up and come into focus. I stopped and stared. The laughter came from the face of a person whose grief was naked to see and yet also alive. They continued to tell their story, as we all do, but their story was interwoven with gratitude, love, forgiveness, and grace.

Tears are unapologetic, as is grief; there was/is no closure, but with the help of others and God the burden became lighter, the valley filled in, and the rough places were made plain. Doors were visible everywhere and my mission became to keep walking because someone was always looking for hope. My spouse Vickie and I eventually found each other on this road, but to understand how we got there we must go back to the beginning.

Chapter 2

The Blue Outfit

I never knew life was a thrill
Well worth my striving for
until
Today.[1]

THE RESPONSIBILITY WAS MINE and proved to be no small hurdle—find the right outfit for Nicholas to wear when he came home from the hospital. Vickie smiled when I showed her the sky blue, one-piece outfit with white trim and buttons up the middle and a zipper in the back. She grinned with that compassionate look that speaks to the deep connection we have shared for a long time. Mission accomplished!

Nicholas and I shared a strong bond from the very beginning. He was born on the first day of August in 1981. The room was noisy; a new life was seeking to enter the world! Watching the doctor ease Nicholas out of the womb was thrilling. When Nicholas was born, the doctor discovered two cysts on Vickie's ovary. All said and done, it seems rather insignificant now, but at the time it was quite scary. She had been awake for the entire birthing procedure, protected from pain by an epidural. As the doctor asked if I would agree to Vickie being put under anesthesia so he could remove the cysts, they handed me the baby. Then they proceeded to complete the surgery.

Once Vickie was cleared of any negative implications, Nicholas and I were moved to a nearby rocking chair, where our relationship was born in a flood of tears, tears of gratitude and hope. I sang to him. "Hush little baby

1. Christensen, *Waves*, 35.

9

don't you cry . . ." And then my own version that I made up on the spot. I couldn't believe that Vickie and I participated in bringing this little life into being.

I called my parents and shared the good news and his name. "Mom and Dad, we have a baby boy. Vickie is fine. His name is Nicholas Alvin and he has big ears just like Grandpa and Dad." I called Vickie's parents and told them the good news and they were ecstatic.

With all the issues of my own upbringing and struggles with my parents, I still wanted, even craved, to be a dad, a father, and to do so with a son (secretly thinking I could do better than my parents). When that little baby came forth from Vickie's womb all covered in blood and fluid, with skin as pink as a beautiful setting sun, my heart leapt for a joy that previously seemed out of reach.

Later, I fetched the car while Vickie and Nicholas were wheeled to the front door of Evanston (Illinois) Hospital. Our car was complete with a new baby seat that swamped our little baby boy. Tucked into the seat with the straps holding him in place, facing forward in the middle of the back seat as was custom in that day, and with Vickie sitting next to him, warrior Dad set out on the first journey as a family, with the responsibility to insure we made it home safely. We did.

Our arrival home was remarkable. Now that Nick was born, Vickie's toxemia disappeared, as did thirty-six pounds. She looked and felt much better. We were both continually ignorant of the responsibility we now had.

Vickie's parents soon joined us. We tried to tell her dad that Nicholas was a beautiful baby, but he wouldn't say a word until he saw him. He thought too many parents say their baby is beautiful only to see that the baby is just "butt ugly." When we all finally met, he saw that Nicholas was, in fact, a beautiful baby, as Vickie's mom knew; and we joyously cried in gratitude.

Their arrival was a blessing. Vickie was still weak from the surgery and her parents jumped right in to caring for our house, for us, and most especially for Nicholas. One of my fondest memories of my mother-in-law, Tix, was her bathing Nicholas when he was newly home. She took what seemed like hours to caress, wash, and dry every inch of his body. Vickie always said of her mom, "She's gonna rub the skin right off of him." The gentleness, care, and love that she showed, however, brought deep joy to all.

In the midst of starting a family, we were also looking for a new place to live in the western suburbs of Chicago. Having accepted a call to start a new church in the Bloomingdale area, we were able to find a rental home in Carol Stream, settled amongst many families with young children, and so began our transition to a new place with new horizons. While the new church was coming along, our finances required that Vickie also return to work outside the home. After some interviewing, she took a part-time position as an insurance claims adjustor with a company in the western suburbs. Our financial margins were so thin that for this to work I would stay with Nicholas one day and then we would see if we could find a sitter for two days a week.

God answered our concern by sending a new church member, Dawn Ruge, into our lives. This was another true blessing. She had a baby boy a few months older than Nicholas and was looking to make some money. Chuckie was her third child, so she also had another quality we desired: experience. Dawn agreed to care for Nicholas two days a week and we were set. Soon, much to my chagrin, Vickie's first day of work quickly arrived, which meant my first day of childcare. We laugh now at my typically male belief that it couldn't be that difficult to manage a child, home, and dinner in one day. That first night of Vickie's work, the meal I had for supper was humble pie. I can't remember what we actually ate. I was so glad to see Vickie come home, realizing I had no idea what it was like to manage a child, run a home, and prepare food. Our lives became full of normal. We worked, we played, and we raised our child.

We were on the five-year plan for children. By the end of 1985, Vickie was pregnant with our daughter Hannah, and we entered into the holidays with life unfolding beautifully. Other voices were clamoring for attention. While our family continued to grow, my own maturity wasn't keeping up. One day that holiday season, while in the old Marshall Field's in Chicago, I placed Nicholas on my shoulders and, looking in a mirror, wondered if this was all there was to life: kids, work, career boredom, married to the same woman, financial stress . . . but mostly kids. Little did I know! Our issues were no different than others'. We had several good friends in the church and beyond, good connections with our extended families, and our lives were rich in many ways, even though doubts sometimes persisted. We were normal!

Chapter 3

April 1, 1986

Have you come to the Red Sea place in your life,
Where in spite of all you can do,
There is no way out, there is no way back,
There is no other way but through?[1]

ONE OF NICHOLAS'S PHYSICIANS said that in 1986 some forty-three children in the United States would be diagnosed with common leukemia marked by what's called "Philadelphia chromosome." Nicholas became one of the forty-three. Nothing in his life to that point prepared us or indicated that he would contract a serious and ultimately fatal disease.

In February of 1986, with Vickie three months pregnant with Hannah, unusual physical experiences began to unfold with Nicholas. He got sick with the flu in March of that year. We didn't think anything of that. Vickie took Nicholas to visit her parents and there was one picture of her, her dad, and Nicholas and you could see he just didn't look right. His face was so sad, and he looked tired. But there was no real cause for alarm. We thought he was perhaps simply feeling the stress of our family at the time. When they returned home later in March, he began to struggle. The tipping point took place at his little preschool, when he fell off the jungle gym. The teachers were so worried that one of the kids had pushed him, but that wasn't the case. He began to complain about his legs hurting. The doctors told us that growing pains were growing pains and that sometimes joints hurt in children as they grow. Little did we know that a pervasive disease was creating tumors that were inhibiting his joints.

1. Flint, *Grace*, 65.

12

We took him to the doctor for a check and, again, they said he had the flu. After a round of antibiotics and acetaminophen, he was back to subnormal. Then one day while Vickie was shopping with Nicholas, he turned ashen white in the cart. She took him to the doctor again. Concerned that he was not well, the doctor wanted to draw some blood. While worried, we still did not think of him as being seriously ill. Then one day, shortly thereafter, he and his little friend Justin joined me at the health club. Nicholas was chasing his friend and just could not keep up. Then I looked at his face. Something wasn't right. His eyes were drooping and his face was swollen. In the meantime, we were called back to the doctor.

When we arrived, no one looked us in the face. Something was terribly wrong with our son. The doctor informed us that Nicholas had significant trouble with his blood and needed to go to Children's Memorial Hospital in Chicago right away. "Go home, pack a bag, and head downtown. Go to the emergency room. They will be waiting for you." I pulled the doctor aside and asked if Nicholas was going to die right now. He responded, "No, but he is very ill and needs to be seen as soon as possible." Panic rose as the lump in my throat threatened to choke off my breathing. Fear poured out of Vickie's eyes.

We made a quick stop at home. After placing two phone calls, one to each set of parents, off we went (no cell phones back then). We had packed a few clothing items for Nicholas and for ourselves. Upon arrival at the hospital we went immediately to the emergency room and were met soon after by a wonderful and kindly doctor who began a diligent process of diagnosis. At first, they thought Nicholas had pneumonia, then perhaps appendicitis; those both proved inaccurate. Finally, after a series of brutal tests, two physicians and several nurses gathered us in an all-white room and explained to us that Nicholas had leukemia. Vickie cried, believing that meant certain death. I got angry and hit the table. Foolish! Selfish! Frightened! Confused!

The doctors explained that it was common leukemia at this point and high risk because of certain factors in his diagnosis and presenting symptoms. They also quickly explained that meant nothing in terms of survival rates. As we listened in shock, the doctors told us treatment would be aggressive, as the disease had permeated his body. However, they were confident he would show immediate signs of improvement and be in remission within four weeks. Treatment was to begin right away. Nicholas was quickly moved to a room on the oncology floor and chemotherapy begun.

The next critical juncture would be after the passage of one month. What we didn't realize at the time was that if he did not get into remission, this type of leukemia was incredibly resilient and current protocols would not work. We simply kept believing and praying that he would enter remission.

Within a week we were back home and into an intense routine of treatment. Some drugs could be administered at home, some at our local well-baby clinic, and some had to be administered at the clinic at Children's Hospital in Chicago. Later, when radiation was added, Nicholas would receive treatment in three different locations on the same day. He was a trooper, but it was often difficult. The treatment for leukemia is needle invasive. He needed a central line, leg shots deep into his thigh tissue, and spinal taps. While there were some drugs available to numb the pain, there were no drugs available to numb his anxiety. That calling fell to his parents. We did whatever it took.

Soon after we arrived home the shock of the direction our life had taken began to wear off. But still, seemingly mundane tasks like taking the trash outside became not so routine. Standing by the trash can one day, I thought that perhaps this was "the" tragedy or trauma that would affect our lives and now having this to experience we would kind of be immune to any more. That was a hope, naive, but still a hope. Immediately the thought struck me that tragedy does not work that way. God does not reflect upon our lives and determine this tragedy here and that tragedy there and state that the Johnson family has had enough. No, shit happens! And God sits with us in the shit.

As the days passed, chemotherapy centered on weekly visits to the oncology clinic at Children's Memorial Hospital. What a world! Every race, age, and disposition of child was present each week for treatment. Our biggest mistake at that time was not putting in a "permanent" central line so Nick didn't need a new IV line each week. Back in those days it meant he couldn't go swimming, or bathe normally, or shower without serious restrictions. In addition, the maintenance of the line required fastidious care on the part of the parents. We figured he would rather have his freedom. We figured wrong. The weekly suffering and fear were almost more than I could handle. He would try to run away from the nurses. I had to catch him, bring him into the room as he whimpered, hold him down while he screamed, and struggle against my own emotional limitations.

One time the doctors talked to us about trying to get him to calm down because his tears, crying, and shouting were affecting the nurses.

With a look of indignation, I stated that it wasn't Nick's job to make them feel good about the pain they were inflicting for his cure, and it was not fair for them to expect that he wouldn't be afraid. The nurses brought in his physician, Dr. Cohn, who also tried to get us to calm him down. I looked at her with "the look" and then a look of sheer resignation, begging her to see that we didn't know what to do ourselves to calm him down. The routine continued weekly for several months.

Prednisone, a steroid, constitutes another component of leukemia treatment. This created a voracious appetite in Nicholas. They suggested we leave a sandwich in the fridge at night and we thought they were joking. We did it but didn't believe that he would get up to eat. They were right. He simply had to eat. Some mornings he would eat four or five eggs with toast and juice. He ate all day. He gained weight, lost his hair, and occasionally got sick from the drugs. One day we were in the cafeteria at Children's Hospital and he was chowing down on a grilled cheese, his second grilled cheese, when he rolled his eyes, tilted his head, and exclaimed, "I think I'm going to throw up!" I jumped to my feet and prepared to catch whatever came forth, then he looked up to me with that beautiful smile of his and said, "Joked ya!" I could have wrung his neck but deeply appreciated the fact that he still had a sense of humor.

Finally, the end of one month came and it was time to test for remission. The test was a painful test called a bone marrow aspirate, where a long needle is inserted into the pelvic bone marrow and marrow is withdrawn and reviewed under the microscope for any evidence of disease. He was in remission and we had successfully navigated the first major hurdle in his treatment. Nicholas was surviving.

It may sound strange to say that we fell into a new routine, but we did. Vickie stepped away from her job. Besides caring for Nicholas, she was now six months pregnant with Hannah. Thankfully, the church was understanding of my need to adjust my schedule weekly, on the fly, in order to handle all the places Nicholas needed to be for treatment. Nick was regularly hospitalized for neutropenia, which was the result of low white cell count, and for the transfusion of blood platelets. We often traveled to Children's for emergency room activity due to bleeding. Whatever it took is what we did.

In the midst of the intense first six months of Nicholas's treatment, our beautiful daughter Hannah was born on August 4. What a great day. Soon though, Hannah came home, and our work became increasingly more intense. Gratefully, Vickie's parents came north and were able to stay with us for a period of time so we could navigate all these huge changes taking place in our lives. By now, Nicholas had some weeks that didn't require several trips for treatment, and we were grateful for that, but when fall came it was back to the intense protocol for another three or four months.

Nick returned to school, as he was able. With the nausea under control, he could go to class but often had to return home because of fatigue, sickness, or treatment. His teachers were incredible. Interestingly Nick later revealed that some parents had shared about his illness with their children, including the fact that he was probably going to die, and his friends told him so at school. I was furious. We chose the path of telling him what was happening and not hedging on all the possibilities. Besides these outliers, his friends were good to him. Our friends were good to him. His family was good to him, and his family was good to each other.

There were some really pleasurable times. One great day was when I went to his class and invited him to leave with me because we were heading to Disney World. He was taken completely by surprise. The group at Children's for granting wishes gave us five days in Florida and away we went, with two kids in tow. I can't remember much about that time except the joy of getting away to a place that was warm and the kindness of people everywhere we went. When we returned home, Nicholas was moving out of the woods and actually into a time of maintenance treatment. By May of 1987 he was, all things considered, in great shape. We were able to plan a summer stay of five weeks at Mackinac Island, Michigan and did so. Packing up early one morning, we headed out for what would be the summer of a lifetime. With Hannah in tow and hope abounding, off we went.

Upon our return home in August, Nicholas got set to return to school. He had been in remission now for more than sixteen months and we were getting optimistic about his chances. We didn't know at the time that the Philadelphia chromosome marked him for death within two years. To this day we have no idea if the research confirmed this at the time or not, or whether we wished to know or not. Perhaps ignorance was bliss. Hard to say! Either way, Nick returned to school in the fall in good shape, if a bit lower on energy than others, and proceeded to have a great fall semester in second grade. Thanksgiving and Christmas were beautiful. And then came January 1988.

New Year's celebrations have always been more emotional and melancholic than other holidays. There was something about beginning the New Year—ending the past year and wondering what the new year would hold for our family. Early in the month we noticed petechia on Nick's legs, little red spots indicating that his blood was not clotting well. We took him to the emergency room for a transfusion. Later, when the spots returned, we scheduled him at the clinic. When we arrived and showed his legs to the doctor, we could tell by her look and the looks of the nurses that we could be looking at relapse. They tested his blood while we waited and paced, our nerves frayed. His attending physician returned all excited and placed the results before us, showing that Nicholas was still in remission. When I looked closely at the name, however, it wasn't Nicholas's. She had brought us the wrong results. When Nicholas's actual results were finally reviewed, she returned, deeply saddened, to share that he had relapsed. We were crushed.

All leukemia patients and their families fear relapse. For Nicholas, relapse meant that the options for cure, longevity, and healing were significantly less than when we started. In this situation research around the Philadelphia chromosome revealed that while a repeat of conventional chemotherapy would "probably" induce a remission, the remission would be for a dramatically shorter duration than the previous one. The alternative was a bone marrow transplant, which in 1988 was still somewhat primitive and only done in three or four hospitals in the United States.

In a perfect world, Hannah, Nick's sister, would have been a perfect match and we would have moved forward with several options. She wasn't. Nor was there any match in the fledgling bone marrow donor pool. That left one option, a mismatched transplant, where one parent or the other, usually the father, is the donor. That was only offered at one hospital in the United States, the University of Iowa Hospitals and Clinics, and with Dr. Michael Trigg, the only physician undertaking such an experimental treatment. Off to Iowa!

We went for an introductory session in February. I couldn't believe that Iowa was the place, but when we drove up to the hospital and their impressive medical facilities it became clear we were going to be in good hands. Dr. Trigg examined Nick and met with us, explaining the procedure and the risks involved. At this point there was only a 10 percent chance that he would survive. That seems so small in hindsight, but at the time it was a substantial hook upon which to place our hopes. Like most parents, we believed that he would be the one in ten; it wasn't a competition, simply an ardent hope. Dr. Trigg explained that before Nick could undergo bone marrow transplant at Iowa he had to get back into remission. Our new short-term goal became a second remission. We returned to our home, aware of the stakes of what we were contemplating and committed to giving Nicholas every chance at life we could give him. With some prayer and some luck, he was in remission, again, within four weeks. Off to Iowa we went.

Transplant procedures take time, generally at least three months. We rented a small apartment in Coralville, Iowa and made that our home for what would turn out to be nearly five months. Once settled, Nicholas was admitted to the hospital, and we were told that under no circumstances save near death would we be able to stay with him. Installed on the pediatric bone marrow floor, at least he was surrounded by kids. Once again, we adjusted to a new life. In the meantime, our daughter Hannah, now nineteen months old, went to live with her grandparents in Arkansas. We struggled with this decision but ultimately decided that she would be more loved and coddled there than we would be able to offer in such a stressful, life-and-death environment. We've wondered many times about the wisdom of that decision, realizing that all of us were doing the best we could at the time with what we had.

In addition to taking time, transplant procedures are incredibly invasive. In Nicholas's case, the plan was a controlled poisoning and destruction of the interior blood-producing systems in his body in anticipation of planting a whole new system. Massive dosages of chemotherapy are administered through IV, into the spine, and through shots. The desire is to kill off the current bone marrow with all its disease and replace it with new and disease-free marrow. At the same time, the total body is radiated, insuring sterility, because the two places leukemia cells hide out in boys are the brain and the testicles. All of that took place within six weeks.

Nicholas was transplanted on April 1, 1988. The marrow was harvested from me early that morning. Needles were inserted into my hip from the front and back and the liquid marrow was removed. As a joke, Dr. Trigg asked me if I wanted to see the marrow. Of course. He lifted up a bag of some kind of green fluid and everyone laughed. I didn't know any better, so I thought maybe the marrow was green. That made them laugh even more. He then went to work adapting the marrow before its insertion into Nick. My parents were there. Friends were there. Everyone was full of hope.

After the marrow is infused into the patient, the next waiting game begins. Marrow is a liquid that enters the body through an IV, settles in the lungs, and then, miraculously, seeks out its particular location in the body, and then settles in to attach and grow. The first threshold is whether the marrow takes hold and finds a home attaching to the bone interiors of the recipient. Next, does the marrow begin to grow and produce the necessary cells to sustain life? In particular the doctor wants to see immune cells, white cells. Sure enough, within ten days cells began showing on Nick's tests and all looked good. There is a disease associated with transplants called graft-versus-host disease, where the new marrow attacks the old body. Medications are necessary to keep that from happening to a large extent. However, some amount of attack is helpful because the leukemia cells are old cells, and the hope is that the new will devour all the old, including any leukemia cells that remain. Nicholas had very little graft-versus-host disease.

Children are so resilient. The atmosphere on the unit was filled with as much fun and joy as was possible in such a life-threatening reality. The kids learned early on how to run around while attached to their IV poles, and all water toys were acceptable on the unit and all employees and patients were equal game, including the doctor.

There was an apocryphal story told of Dr. Trigg. He entered the room of a teenage boy who feigned being sick and, when the doctor approached, the boy pulled out a huge water gun from underneath the covers and blasted away at Dr. Trigg, who only laughed hysterically. The next morning when the patient awoke, he discovered that Dr. Trigg had entered his room as he slept and painted his bald head. Such playfulness helped to ease the tension of the environment.

At the same time, life on the unit was challenging. In the weeks we were at Iowa we met eighteen kids, of whom fifteen died and three went home—one of whom had anemia, not leukemia, and one of whom was Nicholas. The children on the unit were perceptive as to what was at stake, their lives, and the relationships of support they formed. Post-transplant, those who die usually do so from a form of pneumonia that also kills those suffering from AIDS. Children on Nick's floor would move from their room to the pediatric ICU, from where they generally never returned and eventually died.

Nick's friend Cory died. He was a beautiful young boy of twelve who had battled leukemia for five years. One night he went to the ICU and then, within two days, died. We opted to not say anything to Nicholas. When he woke up the next day and went for a stroll around the unit, he noticed that Cory wasn't in his room. He hustled back to his room where Vickie and I were sitting and asked: "Where's Cory?" Reluctant to tell him the truth, I finally said, "He died yesterday." "Why didn't you tell me?" Nicholas shouted.

"He was my friend! Don't ever do that to me again. Don't ever not tell me about what has happened to any of my friends up here." We were shocked. We had no idea how aware he was and how much he was paying attention. Children who face life-threatening illnesses mature at a rate much faster than others; they quickly grasp that they are fighting for their lives. We never did hide any news of other kids from him again! He was young and old and all else.

While all this was unfolding, our new church in Bloomingdale had just completed the first building and a dedication was set for early July. I wanted very much for Vickie to join me, so my parents watched Nick and she flew to Chicago. Severe turbulence rocked the plane the entire trip, while the pilot skirted thunderstorms and made one attempt at landing before being successful with his second try. Vickie's nerves, already frayed by life in Iowa, were shattered. We sat in the Hamlet restaurant trying to eke out a conversation. She wondered if we should get divorced. The stress was overwhelming. The demands of the church kept me away from her. Our ability to cope was evaporating. And our son hadn't even faced the deepest test to date; nor had we. The new church was dedicated as Vickie and I sat, stood, and kneeled in a stupor, aware that our life wasn't here now but was in Iowa and in Arkansas. We returned to Iowa.

Once back, we were soon met with the greatest test to date of the transplant process. Nicholas contracted a virus, a virus that defied recognition and caused fear and trepidation. Test after test revealed that the virus reproduced rapidly and was crowding out his bone marrow and the marrow's capacity to produce good cells. After a week of this, Nicholas stopped eating and drinking and our fear mounted. Physicians tried various options, none of which worked. We tried, I tried, to make him eat. His frustration grew so strong with me that one day as I was trying to get him to eat, he simply jumped up on his bed and shouted at the top of his lungs for the entire unit to hear, "Fuck you, Dad! Fuck you! Leave me alone. I don't want to eat. Quit trying to make me!" And returned to his bed. Time to take a break, I thought, and did. Others thought this funny.

But it wasn't funny. We were losing him; he was dying. As it turned out, he had contracted a form of the virus called Epstein-Barr, which generally presents as mono but in his case presented as an undifferentiated virus. We had dear Anne, the chaplain, come in to lay hands on him for healing and to listen as we cried out our fears and anxieties. Nicholas remained silent. Dr. Trigg entered and suggested we try a drug called alpha interferon.

We agreed. Within days the virus slowed down and Nicholas's body began to fight it on its own. The treatment continued for weeks and finally he turned the corner. Nicholas was not only alive, but we were about to finally go home and return to Bloomingdale.

When the day finally came in August, we packed up all our gear and headed home. With fear, hope, and relief, and surrounded by love, we made our way out of the intense and focused world of transplant and back into the world of the everyday. Nicholas was met by friends and caring people with signs and gifts and good wishes. He was very overweight due to the steroids and had to wear a mask for protection against disease, but the homecoming warmed his heart and ours.

With a seriously compromised immune system, he could not return to public school. Eventually, to help him along and to respect the need to protect his immune system, we hired a dear tutor named Ann Marriotti. She came by the house twice a week to work with Nick. He soared academically. The school allowed him to bring a computer home and all the books he needed, and he went to work quickly surpassing his classmates in mastering second grade. I returned to work. Vickie managed our home and Nick's daily care, including IVs and all. Hannah returned home in August and we tried, for the third time in less than three years, to adapt to another new way of living, a new normal.

Chapter Four

The Unimaginable

> I could see you and Mom crying as I was dying. I know you wanted to help me, but this last step, well this last step I had to take on my own. And because of your love, I could.[1]

WHEN OCTOBER OF 1988 rolled around it was time for a three-month checkup in Iowa. So far, all things looked to be going well. Remembering that Nick was one of only three of eighteen who had actually made it home, we were cautiously optimistic. We left for Iowa again, naturally apprehensive. But our fears were allayed upon completion of his last test, a bone marrow transplant test. We returned home with the news that all was as it should be, the new marrow was mine, and he was recovering well. We were ecstatic.

The next evening, just as I was preparing to leave for a church meeting, we received a phone call from Dr. Trigg. As a normal part of the procedure they take the residue in the bone marrow test tube, solidify it, slice it, and look closely at it under the microscope. There they discovered four leukemia cells similar to the previous ones. Vickie, who had taken the call, was panicked. She exclaimed out loud, "What does this mean? Is it back? Is it back? Is he going to die?" Dr. Trigg, honest as he had always been, said yes it was back and yes, he was probably going to die.

We were devastated. We had traveled from the top of the mountain of joy and hope to the deepest valley of despair and death in less than twenty-four hours. We had to wait two weeks before the news could be confirmed. The date would be November 29, 1988.

---

1. Nicholas, my imagining.

The two weeks of waiting wore all of us down. We brought our parents and family into the loop of what we were facing. People were praying from coast to coast. "Forever Young" by Rod Stewart played as we drove to the clinic on November 29. And once again, and now for what would be the last time, Dr. Cohn told us that the leukemia was back. By now, Nicholas was well aware of the conditions. I held him in the car before we went in for the test and he asked if he was having another bone marrow test. I said yes. He asked if the leukemia was back. I said I thought so. He asked if he was going to die. Time stopped as I held him, one of those moments when one ponders the virtue of telling the truth or attempting a distraction; I told the truth. I said, "Yes, you are going to die." He might as well hear it from his dad who loves him than from anyone else. Our tears and our love were our consolation. Slowly we entered the clinic prepared to embrace the final test.

There were choices. There are always choices. We could have begun chemo again right away. Remission was almost assured but so was a quick relapse. We could transplant him again, but 100 percent of children transplanted within a year died from the second transplant due to the effects of the chemicals more than anything else. Or we could enjoy what time we had with him and help him to enjoy that time as well. We had one week to decide.

On the day we were to travel to Children's Hospital with our decision, I came into the kitchen and found Nick sitting on Vickie's lap. She was gently weeping. I said, "He doesn't want any more treatment, does he?" She shook her head. "He is afraid we will get mad at him, but he's tired, and his body hurts, and he doesn't want to go through that again with no hope of living longer."

I've often wondered since then about the wisdom he had and our trust in that wisdom. We certainly as his parents could have overpowered his decision and made him receive treatment again, but that would have been against his wishes. Is it possible that a seven-year-old could know more about himself and his body and his life than his parents? Yes! We sat together, the three of us, and then Hannah, and had a good cry as we accepted, reluctantly, a decision that was, in the final analysis, a decision to allow Nick's life to take its own course. These many years later I look at pictures of him and see the youth that had become invisible as he aged in treatment. Did I lose perspective? I don't think so.

And yet, it was difficult for me to let go and believe that we had such limited options. I got on the phone and called around the world to the best minds that I could find. They all answered and they all, once they heard Philadelphia chromosome, metaphorically shook their heads and said there was nothing more they could do than what was offered by Iowa and Chicago. The kind and wise doctor at M. D. Anderson clinics in Texas apologized. He understood our pain and fear and grief and said he wished that there was something they could do, but research hadn't taken them that far. He was sorry. That was, interestingly enough, soothing.

We informed our family of what was unfolding and asked my dad if he could make arrangements for Nick and me to fly to Florida on one of the Ingram corporate jets. The next day we dealt with our grief by heading to Florida. Nick got to pilot the plane and we got four days of warmth and sunshine, baseball, and Disney World. We had a blast and enjoyed our time together. When we returned home, reality hit and the mild depression began to seep into our hearts, into my heart. Nick was ecstatic with his decision and that did bring comfort to us. We enjoyed Christmas that year as our entire family gathered to tell him how much we loved him.

My mother, God love her, and obsessed as she was with giving all grandchildren the same thing, had purchased savings bonds for her grandkids. They all opened the bonds and Nicholas asked out loud, "What's this, Dad?" "It's a savings bond." "How does it work?" "Well in seven years it will be worth $50." "But I'll be dead before then." I thought my mother was going to pass out. The room went quiet. I said, "Yes, that's true. How about if I buy it from you and you can go spend the money?" "That sounds great, Dad. Thanks." Out of the mouths of babes!

Christmas was melancholic and New Year's was joyful and sad. Nicholas was so happy that it was difficult to not be happy for him. Between some pain meds and some mild chemo, he was able to stay active. We would do something special every day, including a wonderful last trip to Arkansas to see his grandparents, fish, eat tater tots, shoot guns, and all. The courage of this young child continues to baffle me to this day—his willingness to embrace his life lived as fully as possible. Some days I'd say to him that he would be okay and be in heaven and he'd say to me, "That's fine but I won't be with you and Mommy!" And that was true, and my heart would break in two and I would see him again as the seven-year-old boy he was.

I took him out and taught him to drive a car and how to drink beer. We even smoked a cigar, although he didn't really like that. His wish was to meet the Chicago Bears and attend a game, and we did that, the infamous Fog Bowl of 1988 against the Philadelphia Eagles.

As February unfolded, Nick clearly began to succumb to the disease. His energy decreased, as did the number of hours he was awake. His world shrank and his own fears and frustrations grew. It seemed easier to be dying when death seemed days away, much more difficult when "terminal episodes" began to take place.

Vickie and I wanted very much to have a conversation with him about the end of his life. He said that he would talk only when he was ready and not a minute before then. We agreed. He was in the hospital at one point in February in need of blood and other chemicals to balance his life, when all of a sudden one night he was ready to talk about his death. Question one: "Dad, can I be buried in the backyard?" "Nick, we aren't allowed to bury you there, but your mom and I will be buried with you, so you are not alone." "Dad, will you remember my birthday?" "Yes, I promise we will have a party every year on your birthday just for you and to remember you." "Dad, will you make sure to tell Sissy and any more children you and Mom might have about me?" "Yes, Nicholas, you are always, and always will be, an important part of our family." The conversation was over. We would never talk about these subjects again. Within less than three weeks he would be dead, and the circle of people who knew him and loved him would be left to try and piece our lives back together.

Death approached gradually. Three weeks before Nicholas died our dear friend, Fr. Roy Hendricks, and his wife, Marian, came to visit and to anoint Nick for death and burial. Nicholas had accompanied me, at his request, to anoint a man who was dying just three weeks before Roy's visit. Now, while Nick was drugged on morphine for the pain and calling out for his mother repeatedly throughout the day, Roy and Marian entered our home with a grace and faith that invited us to take deep breaths and relax. We shared a meal and conversation and then went into the room for his anointing. Roy had brought a little Snoopy doll and placed that on the pillow next to Nick. Then he took his oil and instead of trying to put it on Nicholas's forehead, he just made the sign of the cross on the hand he was holding and asked Jesus to draw him home and heal his wounded and diseased body. This released all the pent-up grief and fear within both Vickie and me. We cried uncontrollably and were held by Roy and Marian until the last tear cascaded down our faces and some sense of balance was restored. The tears were refreshing. Then, abruptly, it was time for them to go. Roy stopped at the door and said a prayer and blessed our house. Everyone slept well that night.

The day before Nick died was classic. First, he wanted to sit on his Papaw's lap. Then he sat next to his Mamaw. He wanted to hold Sissy, although he didn't have the strength. We helped him. He sat with me as we watched Providence play Georgetown in basketball. Then his mom lay down with him, and finally we took him back to his room. His farewell tour was complete.

That evening Nicholas entered into the last few hours of his life. We had kept an attentive vigil with him and while aware he was going to die, we had little idea what to look for in terms of physical indications. While sitting in his room that evening, I noticed a change in his breathing and went to get Vickie. He was dying and we didn't know what to do. After sitting with him for thirty minutes or so, we called our friend, parishioner and hospice nurse Cheryl, and she came over as soon as possible.

Nicholas was beginning to choke to death on his own fluids. Choking is one physical reaction that causes me intense anxiety, so watching this unfold while trying to keep my emotions under check was exhausting, not to mention Vickie and I seeking to comfort each other. Early on, small doses of the drug Ativan proved to be helpful in easing his choking, but then the death rattles came and with them increased suffering. Cheryl left the room after telling us she was going to call the hospice doctor. I learned that I could end his life if the suffering became intolerable: simply hold down the morphine pump button for thirty seconds. It was about 2:45 AM on March 18 and we had been in this tense space for more than three hours.

Wringing hands; racing heart; rocking back and forth against the wall as he choked to death right in front of my eyes. Where was she? Where is Cheryl? The button sat there glaring at me, the button I could push to put him out of his suffering. Hold for the count of thirty! My hands couldn't move. We put dogs to sleep for less.

Cheryl shot into the room, prescription bag in her hand; right to work in a room of pacing, crying, angry, terror-stricken people wanting this absurdity to end. Confidently removing the loaded syringe her hands fumbled as she attached the syringe of Ativan. She looked at me with my arms wrapped so tightly around myself that I could hardly breathe, tears cascading uncontrollably, head shaking back and forth desperately trying to grasp what was unfolding. As she looked at me her eyes said, "You know what's going to happen when I give this to him?" I looked at Vickie. She nodded. "Yes," I said, "Yes, Yes, Yes, please," choking on each word.

She slowly released the drug and with that released all of us. His breathing became lighter, shallow, angel's breath. No movement. Quiet. Measuring seconds in between breaths. Then silence. Then death. Then a collective sigh too deep for words. Then shouts of grief and tears of sadness. Our hearts had broken in two. Thank God for Cheryl. We held Nicholas. Then we washed his body, lit a candle, and anointed him with oil. We sat still and quiet before the chaos unfolded of informing, planning, celebrating, and more.

We stepped into the room where Vickie's parents were sleeping and told them, inviting them to come view Nick's body. They did, and they cried. We woke Hannah and brought her in. What a dream daughter caught in a sophisticated web of grief and loss. Hal, Linda, John, and Christine Toberman came over as soon as Nicholas died. John, who was an incredible friend to Nicholas, asked me to call him when Nicholas died, and I did. We sat the vigil of grief and adaptation. Hal and Linda spent a lot of time with Vickie's parents. As you will read later, they continued to be incredible companions along the way. Finally, finally, we called Chris at the funeral home and he came and took Nick's body. Vickie and I each took a sleeping pill and went to bed.

Later that day, March 18, we awoke to the next day of our lives. After coffee and conversation, Vickie and I decided to head to Springhill Mall for some reason. We went shopping and nearly bought many clothes we didn't need. We were like zombies. We went to Houlihan's for a burger and when I sent it back for the third time I realized that burger would never be right. We just ate what was in front of us, aware that grief shattered whatever good judgment we had.

When we returned home it was time to plan. My parents and family came over. We agreed to have the visitation on Monday and the funeral on Tuesday. It was Holy Week, but I took Palm Sunday off. Friends came by and we put the service together. A thousand people came to the visitation on Monday. We felt so loved and uplifted and exhausted. Family came in from everywhere—from Arkansas, Oklahoma, Florida, and places all around. The memories are a blur really. One memory remains to this day: the entire congregation packed into this new church with tears flowing down our cheeks and arms upraised singing "And I Will Raise Them Up." With our tears and our arms, we weren't simply pleading for Nicholas and my family, we were pleading for all of life, for our lives. We lifted ourselves to God in desperation, hope, and love because at some level we all knew that we had nowhere else to turn. People tell me the service was beautiful in its own way with communion and more singing and balloons and a wonderful reception at Indian Lakes sponsored by my parents.

When the funeral ended and the colored balloons rose into the dazzling bright sky, my son's body tucked inside the hearse, and me thinking it's time to go to the reception, Fr. Hendricks (aka Holy Joe) grabbed me by the arm and said, "Come on, honey! We follow our dead!" This dear man who walked with my family and me for over a year, who would tread the desperate path of grief with me the rest of his life and beyond, who gave us hope that new life could follow such a loss, whose own son John had died from cancer thirty-five years ago, and who had lived to love and heal again, became a lifeline for survival.

The silent ride to the crematorium didn't take long, feelings long ago having succumbed to numbness. The entrance looked like any other well-maintained cemetery. We entered the decorated reception area graciously greeted by the professional death merchants complete with the well-seasoned aura of sympathy. "We will be going with the body to the oven," Roy said. The manager sat stunned. The funeral director's head snapped up. "What?" I wondered silently. "Are you sure?" queried the funeral director and crematory manager in unintended unison. "Yes!" Roy asked, "Are you ready to cremate him now?" "Yes."

We drove to the back. Roy and I drew out Nicholas's casket and placed it on a gurney. We entered an immaculately clean hallway. Two other bodies awaited cremation off to the side wrapped in white cloths. The hallway consisted of painted concrete block walls and sparkling clean tile floor. The color was white, the lighting was bright. The smell of clean permeated our senses, a respectful clean. The temperature was cool but not air-conditioned cool.

Our journey was about fifty feet to the three ovens. The manager opened the door on oven two. Inside was an efficient technological means of destruction. Multiple gas jets surrounded a steel grate sitting on top of finely chosen rock capable of absorbing temperatures up to 2,000 degrees, allowing fire to completely enfold the casket.

All others stepped aside. Roy and I lifted Nick's casket and placed one edge on the steel grate and pushed him in. Tears and snot everywhere. We closed the door. I pushed the button. The roar of the jets began as we stood in silence then shuffling outside for the silent ride back to the reception. Holy Joe looked at me and said, "Honey, we follow our dead!"

Chapter 5

Earthquake and Aftershocks

Traumatic events overwhelm the ordinary systems of care that give people a sense of control, connection, and meaning.[1]

WHAT HAPPENS WHEN A young child dies; what happens, for that matter, when any child dies? My son Nicholas's death shook my world like an earthquake. When he died something shifted dramatically at the epicenter of my being. The intensity of the shock shattered my very soul. Though the quake appeared in one place, the epicenter was somewhere near my core. As is true in a real earthquake, the epicenter isn't always directly connected to where the most destruction takes place. At the actual moment Nicholas died, the location of the greatest destruction internally remained hidden. When heart and life and faith and hope all began to shift and shake and break, all sorts of places of the heart were displaced and destroyed. For a brief moment (who knows when and how long that moment actually lasts; it could be weeks, months, or years), the shaking stopped, and I breathed a sigh of relief thinking perhaps the worst was over.

When I looked around it became apparent that the landscape had been forever changed. While I could not see the very place where the tectonic shift happened, I saw the effects on the surface of my life and on the lives of those connected in any way to Nicholas. Sometimes it takes awhile for the true nature of the damage to be revealed or seen. My eyes only wanted to see what had been normal, not the loss; only to look and see the familiar. But one cannot imagine back into reality the living essence of someone who has died. The damage is permanent, as in an earthquake. Even though

1. Herman, *Trauma*, 33.

29

some things may get repaired, they are never the same . . . and we hunger for things to return to the same.

One outcome of an actual earthquake is a tsunami, a towering wave of water that threatens everything in its path. The image is a focused metaphor that captures my early feelings of grief after Nick's death. Wave after wave of sadness, anger, and grief washed over my family, friends, others affected by the tragedy, and me. The wave threatened all of us with the possibility of drowning in despair and hopelessness. Technically the tsunami is an aftershock and only becomes apparent to those who have traveled the pathway and have an emotional connection with the beautiful child that died. I showed up publicly at the events around the death of Nicholas while at the same time grasping for air to breathe and a lifeline to lift me out of the drowning waters of loss. I tried to hold on to objects to keep from being swept away in the tsunami of feelings, only to discover, that as with a real tsunami, the waves were much more powerful than my ability to hold on. Sometimes, as a dear monk once advised, one simply gets swept up in the water and surrenders to the flow of the water as well as the flow of life. Water moves down. I was carried into the valley of the shadow of death. Easy way down; tough way back out!

The emotional tsunami further reminded me that life was out of control. Things were simply happening at a pace that left me in the dust of human existence. The uncontrolled events led me to protest my previous belief that I controlled events. Before the death of Nicholas, I was able to convince myself that providence was actually mine to possess. Not anymore, not after that day. I didn't control waves of grief that lived beyond my reach and control; they came at all times and in all manners of expression: wave after wave after wave. Eventually the waves got smaller and repeated less often, but by then Vickie and I were completely exhausted and aware that the new trajectory of our life was set in a direction guided by grief, at least for now.

And then came the aftershocks, the further losses that get compounded upon the original loss, making the grief nearly unbearable. Aftershocks can appear near the epicenter or miles away. They are of less intensity yet often cause even more damage because the initial earthquake has weakened the original structures. Most outsiders cannot observe the aftershocks.

My internal "structures" were weak, and yet the aftershocks continued long after Nicholas died. The aftershocks took many forms. First there was the second wave of awareness that my child was dead, and the reality I would never see Nick in this life in the flesh again. Then came the aftershock captured by the fact that when he died, some dreams of my life died as well; not all of them, but many. I had a vision, an idea, of how life would live out. The death of Nick altered that dream. Yet you will hear that the vision of life changed and a rich life with Hannah and Zachary, seeing them off to college, married, adding to our family all helped to remind me of a larger vision of life.

In the moment, however, when a prolonged illness is involved, one parent or the other has given up their lives in service of their child who is now dead. Vickie cared for Nicholas day in and day out for years. She initially lost purpose, meaning, and passion.

Added to these aftershocks came confusion on where to look for stability. Where would I find the anchors in the midst of continuously shaking ground, clouds of dust, insecure footsteps, and frayed emotions? Some friends moved closer and some moved further away because the pain and uncertainty of this kind of loss inhibited their ability to continue to relate. Some were simply afraid and thought that if they hung with me as a bereaved parent (and a priest by God), they, too, might lose a child. While my religious community and God would prove critical down the road, in the moment of the tsunami neither proved particularly helpful. Sometimes those of us who lose a child also lose God, because whatever we believed about God was shattered when the child died.

The list of aftershocks goes on and on. More often than not they weren't as painful as the original loss. But they did contribute to the challenge of healing, particularly, because my own personality and psychological infrastructure had been weakened by this loss. I was extremely vulnerable. The original quake weakened my ability to cope, grow, learn, and heal. Each aftershock weakened the superstructure of the self and increased my vulnerability. I had no power over the shocks unless I anesthetized myself and chose to disengage from reality (always a creative choice). Nevertheless, the aftershocks kept hammering away at my previous life, deconstructing reality in order to further the necessary work of grief and healing.

We can begin the healing process when we know and accept all that's been damaged by the earthquake, and we know that only when all the aftershocks have calmed in frequency and intensity can we take stock of ourselves. Like on a submarine after an attack. The commander asks that all areas check in with a damage control report. They never ask until the ship is stable, and all effects of torpedoes or depth charges have ceased. The same is true for our aftershocks. They could go on for some time. Once they are over, we can then begin the slow and arduous process of assessing the damage.

All earthquakes involve a tectonic shift in the earth's underground structure. What might appear as a slight shift in formation can bring catastrophe somewhere on the surface. Nothing returns to its original place. All earthquakes begin somewhere. Earthquakes involving grief begin and find their intensity with love. And so this story continues, with love.

For some reason the emotional experience of an earthquake, tsunami, and aftershocks brought to mind the challenges of deciding which path to take by choice, by divine guidance, by experience, or by emotional need. Robert Frost's poem encapsulates where I stood:

> I shall be telling this with a sigh
> Somewhere ages and ages hence:
> Two roads diverged in a wood, and I,
> I took the one less traveled by,
> And that has made all the difference.[2]

No one road captures the journey of grief and as this portion suggests, often I looked and wondered about the road chosen after Nicholas died. Many potential "roads" followed Nicholas's death. As noted before, initially I made choices out of death, desperation, and denial; later the choices were made out of hope, need, uncertainty, confusion, guilt, faith, and love. So many roads. Life presented me choices; some I sought while others came my way uninvited. Forces greater than any one person, forces like life and death, love and hate, hope and despair, moved me along, suggesting paths we thought might make us feel at home. And yet, as Frost recognized, we come to realize the uniqueness of paths chosen.

The most famous road in tragedy is the "Why Street." I didn't want to give the "why" question any time but that proved impossible. "Why" is a path, a road. Why did this happen to my son? Why did this happen to us? To me? Why, God?

I remember a friend I'll call George. George enters his doctor's office and discovers his PSA is over 7. The doctor tells him that there are a variety of things this might mean, including prostate cancer. The doctor outlines a series of steps to take in order to determine what is taking place and what treatment, if any, is warranted. George takes his wife, Martha, along with

---

2. Frost, *Mountain Interval*, 1.

him for this initial visit because he's naturally afraid. After the appointment, they meet a close friend for lunch and George immediately tells his friend that he has cancer, and he will probably need surgery and that he might not be able to have sex again. Martha listens in astonishment because that's not what the doctor said at all. When they return home, she asks him what he heard the doctor say. Given more time to travel down this particular road, George says that the doctor told him he has cancer and he better get his affairs in order. Martha replies that he said no such thing. George argues. Martha, remaining calm and centered, reaffirms what she knows to be an accurate portrayal of the appointment. George leaves the room in a huff and goes for a long walk. Martha waits.

Over an hour later George returns home and humbly asks Martha if they can talk. He asks her to recount what she heard earlier at the doctor's office. She reports nearly verbatim what the doctor said. George asks if she's sure and she shows him her notes. She asks him what's going on with him. And this is what George says: "I've lived with the fear of dying and of cancer for years, almost to the point of believing that cancer is inevitable for me. The minute he said my PSA was 7 my mind clicked onto that road I've held for a long time; I immediately raced down the path of illness, pain, suffering, and death. I got to the end of that path before any other information could enter my consciousness, so I could only hear myself, and the loudest voice was my fear. I had no ability, and may not even now, to come back to the start and explore what this means with an open mind devoid of the overwhelming fear. My world collapsed and 'why me' echoed throughout my mind. 'How do I tell the kids? How will you survive? What do I tell my co-workers?'" He began to cry.

Martha walks over and sits down next to him. Taking his hand, she asks if he would like to hear her notes about the appointment. She gently brings him back down the path and repeats for him what had actually been said. George notes that he wants to go back to the doctor and listen again. Martha says she has already made the appointment.

I recall the night Nicholas was diagnosed with leukemia. My mind traveled down many roads very quickly. Vickie's mind traveled right to death. But then our doctors brought us back to reality. All of the roads we imagined were possible, but the path we needed to choose in that very moment centered on the possibility of healing versus not healing. We chose healing. The other roads remained options; and when we finally traveled the road of his death, that road less traveled, we never walked alone.

Within about eighteen months of Nicholas's death, we bought a new swing set and placed it in our backyard in Barrington. While talking with friends on our patio I looked over to my left and saw my beautiful Hannah hanging upside down from the trapeze bar. I panicked. Fear enveloped me from head to toe, inviting me to shout in what would inevitably sound like an angry taunt, "Get down from there!" But I didn't. Instead, I ran smack into the fear, which would become a new friend for a long time.

When I looked at Hannah I knew right then that a critical choice sat in front of me: live out of fear and project that fear all over this young child, or face the fear and embrace the desire for her to live as fearlessly as possible. I smiled and turned away, grateful. Hannah was, and is, courageous. An old road revisited. The road of fear and love. And yet, a new road to come. One of love and joy in time. All in time.

Chapter 6

Marriage

Bless them in their work and in their companionship,
in their sleeping and in their waking,
in their joys and in their sorrows,
in their life and in their death.[1]

VICKIE WAS BORN IN Rockford, Illinois and raised in Corning, Arkansas. She is the second child of Tix and Jimmy Arnold, and has one brother, Steve. Her parents walked out of their high school graduation and over to the parsonage at the Methodist Church and got married. Corning is a small, rural farming community. Vickie's graduating class from high school numbered ninety-six and she was one of the stars. Her parents were prosperous. Their first business was Jimmy's Drive-in. After years of hard work, they sold the business and eventually started Arnold Brothers Building Supply, which they ran for years. Jimmy and his brother, Freddy, together with their dad, Walter, began buying up land and building houses. They financed them and carried all the paper. They were jokingly considered local land barons.

Vickie has always been a lover; she's a walking, talking hug. Our hearts were broken three times with Nicholas. The first time took place when he was diagnosed with leukemia. The second time was when he relapsed. The third time was when he died. And yet throughout, the image of her laying on Nick's left side with her right arm draped over his head and her left holding his hand for hours on end—this is the lens through which to know Vickie and the emptying of herself that she gave for Nicholas.

Vickie has always been a beautiful woman inside and outside. She loved Nicholas to the core and did everything for him that was possible.

1. *Book of Common Prayer*, 430.

There were limits. For one thing, she was pregnant with Hannah when Nicholas became ill. Vickie was and always has been the emotional anchor of our marriage. Not so much in the practical sense, but in terms of staying in the present moment regarding what is unfolding. Whenever she wandered from the present she would begin to cry, fighting her core belief that Nicholas would die and soon.

I was born on the South Side of Chicago. I'm the third of four children to Al and Eileen Johnson. After serving forty-nine months in the Navy in World War II, my dad returned home. My parents were married in May of 1946. My dad was a banker, serving his entire career at the First National Bank of Chicago (now a part of Chase), where he retired as a Senior Vice-President. He loved numbers, music, his family, and Jesus. He also made the decision early in life that he would not be poor.

My Mom was born in Downers Grove, Illinois, a western suburb of Chicago. She trained in her younger life to be a nurse and enjoyed that calling immensely. Mom later took a job at the First National Bank of Chicago and ended up in the department handling the check-in at the end of the day for all tellers (my dad was a teller at this time). She kept finding errors in his reporting at the end of the day. The legend lives in our family that he wasn't making that many mistakes, but she used this as a way of getting his attention. The rest is history.

Imagine the day when a young man from Chicago meets the rural family of Vickie from Corning, Arkansas, population 3,200. For my parents this was a collision. For me, I loved every bit of a new and different culture of which I knew nothing. Her family loved and accepted me and us, even though I was a Yankee.

Vickie and I met on January 24, 1973. One afternoon she left the University of Arkansas in Fayetteville, Arkansas with a group of friends from her hometown for dinner. After dinner, on a fluke, they decided to drive to Tulsa for fun. Two of the guys in the car were members of the Lambda Chi Alpha fraternity and I was one at the University of Tulsa. They decided to come to our house. There I stood in my blue jeans, white T, a pack of Winston's under my sleeve, in an elbowless terry cloth bathrobe, and holding a bowl of ice cream when there was a knock on the door. The door opened to reveal this beautiful woman with incredible eyes and long eyelashes. She batted her eyes and said, "Hi, I'm Vickie. We're from Arkansas and we came here to party!" We were married three years later.

Vickie and I married young. We were emotionally fused and struggled with the idea of how to create emotional distance within our marriage. When Nick got sick we could have easily gone in the direction of separation, but we didn't. The memory of that first night at Children's Hospital remains emblazoned in my mind and heart. That night we both slept in Nicholas's room. The nurses gave him something to help him sleep. The large bed swamped his little body with such droopy eyes and lumpy skin. The room held four beds. Nick's bed was crowded next to a table. An old-fashioned TV rested on metal rods connected to the wall, such that Nick could look up to the TV. He had the bedside remote control, but it was awkward and difficult for him to manage. He wasn't interested.

Vickie "slept" that first night in bed with Nicholas. She didn't sleep. I "slept" in a chair. I didn't sleep. When the sun came up on April 2, 1986, we had no idea what turns, what road or roads, our lives were about to take. No idea at all! We were afraid, vulnerable, alone, somewhat deaf. We were walking on thin ice. We prayed but we hadn't even begun to think about God. Further, Nicholas began chemotherapy that day, and because Vickie was pregnant she needed to stay at a safe distance.

Clearly, instead of going our own ways, we accepted and embraced our love for Nick, and each other, by giving him the best chance possible to live. The focus moved off of our marriage and onto supporting him and then Hannah and then Zachary. We traveled two parallel paths. One was to maintain our relationship and the other was to support our children in very stressful times. Honestly, I was the most selfish partner in our marriage. I still am today, but nothing like back then.

As I write this, Vickie and I have been married for more than forty-five years. I often say that we've had four marriages with the same person and no divorce. (The courtship, the marriage and parenting, careers and parenting, empty nest and retirement, older years. Each is an overlapping stage.) I've learned as a priest over the years that marriages go through stages just like everything else. Stages require renegotiating and basically three pathways present themselves. Pathway one involves the two people taking an honest assessment of their marriage and choosing to work out their differences and thereby deepen their love. A second pathway involves staying in the marriage but slowly beginning to take on behaviors that serve as anesthesia. The third pathway involves renegotiating by getting a divorce. For some reason presenting this context helps share the story of Vickie's and my marriage, most especially dealing with the death of our son.

Recently, still, a friend posted on Facebook how miraculous our marriage survival was considering "something like 90% of all couples losing a child end up getting a divorce." In fact, The Compassionate Friends noted in 2016 that somewhere around 16 percent divorce and most of those divorce for other reasons.[2] All this is to say that Vickie and I were not, and are not, outliers. We fit the norm not the exception, and the norm required work. We didn't get to the place of healing without addressing the pain. We had traveled as far as we could and then eventually needed help.

Our marriage today looks nothing like our marriage in 1989. Thank God! Our love today draws from each other, God, Hannah and Ben, Zachary and Katy, and the deaths of our parents, and Vickie's brother, and our experience with Nicholas; it draws from the mystical presence of the communion of saints. We had the choice to grow together and we did. However, our marriage challenges intensified. When a relationship is emotionally fused, one partner automatically seeks the other partner to fill them up with love. But what happens when one partner is empty, completely consumed with heartbreak? Nothing blessed our marriage more than the discovery that we both grieved differently and that neither had much left over to give the other. This proved frustrating to both of us, and yet the reality of grieving separately pushed us apart just enough to let our marriage mature along with us; we learned another way to be married.

Most importantly, we needed to make sure we didn't overload each other with ridiculous expectations. We also needed to first of all acknowledge our differences and then, rather than see them as marriage weaknesses, we needed to view these differences for the uniqueness they generate. This was a first for Vickie and me. Dr. Charles Alcorn was the therapist we were seeing when we sought to bring balance back to our marriage. He saw us through Nick's illness, death, and our first steps in recovery. He provided two incredible gifts to us. First, he helped us to understand what it means to grieve differently and how to learn our own unique means of grieving. Second, he prayed with us; he brought God to us.

We were unable to place ourselves into God's hands. My vocation became willful, meaning that I worked because that was how I provided for my family, but the vitality of faith had disappeared. Dr. Alcorn simply held our hands at the end of each session, slowly inviting God into our yearning to be healed individually and as a married couple and as a family. Vickie and I cried every time. When we moved to Barrington, our sessions slowly

2. The Compassionate Friends, *Marriage Study.*

came to an end, with Vickie and me more in touch with each other and with our marriage. We weren't healed or whole, but we were committed and together. And as to Charlie? Well, our third child is named Zachary Charles Johnson in gratitude for Dr. Charles Alcorn.

In bereavement one area of continual mystery centers on anniversaries. One Sunday morning in 1994 we were having brunch after church at the local diner with Hannah and Zachary. The check came, and Hannah, who was eight at the time, offered to pay. She had a whole bag of coins. I had no idea where she found all that money, but I wasn't overly concerned. A few days later I opened my chest, looked at my change jar, and noticed that someone made a considerable withdrawal. During that same week Vickie and Hannah visited a Christian bookstore. When they stopped later for a treat, Vickie noticed Hannah had several items that she hadn't purchased. She had shoplifted. Vickie calmly asked Hannah if she had taken the things and she said yes. They returned to the store and Hannah returned the items to the clerk with her apology. What was going on?

Family emotional systems teaches that when a child begins to show unusual behaviors they are probably triangulated with some issue with their parents.[3] I wondered. In the meantime, Vickie and I had begun seeing an incredible therapist named Elizabeth Pannier. Elizabeth was a quiet, centered woman. Her office reflected a space of life and spirit. We went to her because after five or so years we were stuck in processing our grief and in learning how to be present for the other person. The levels of loss were deepening. The struggle to move on with our lives professionally and personally was overwhelming. And besides, we were coming up on an anniversary.

Nicholas lived 2,755 days, or seven years, eight months, and eighteen days. Our anxiety intensified as Hannah approached this number. Frankly I didn't want to say anything to Elizabeth because I thought we were being paranoid. There was nothing to suggest Hannah wouldn't make it alive to the day 2,756. She was in great health and under a good doctor's care. As it turned out, Hannah's behavior paralleled our increased anxiety. Once we explored our fears and were able to embrace them, we lightened up; and we never had another incident with Hannah. We had talked to her, of course, and asked about her behavior and listened. She couldn't express why but we knew why. We learned that along the way of grief, Vickie and I would need to keep in touch with the mysterious ways grief affected our family. Hannah immediately calmed down. We all did.

3. Friedman, *Generation*, 36.

Chapter 7

Family

... who settest the solitary in families:
We commend to thy continual care
The homes in which thy people dwell.
... Turn the hearts of the parents to the children,
And the hearts of the children to the parents ...[1]

IN 1996 VICKIE, HANNAH, Zachary, and I presented ourselves before Fr. Scott Hunter for the laying on of hands for healing. The first seven years since Nick's death had taken their toll and Vickie and I were exhausted with the emotional ashes of death, life, new birth, vulnerability, fear, and love. We had been married twenty years at that point and had survived ministry, the death of a child, Vickie's return to work, a move, the births of Hannah and Zachary, and so much more. But in our souls we were hurting. We were still trying to draw our complete selves into the present and knew, instinctually, that healing was the key. Healing prayers could not come at a better time.

All four of us approached the kneeling station. We knelt together and noticed that the other stations had all gone quiet and all attendees at the service were looking at our family. All four of us knelt together before Scott, who marked us each with holy oil and said the ancient words of healing and particular prayers for each of us and for our family. "I lay my hands upon you and anoint you with oil in the name of the Father, and of the Son, and of the Holy Spirit; beseeching the mercy, grace, and love of our Lord Jesus

---

1. *Book of Common Prayer*, 828.

Christ, that he may restore you to fullness of health in mind, body, and spirit."[2]

All of us were crying, Vickie and I because we were so thirsty for healing, Hannah because she knew enough about loss to understand the desire for healing as a family, and Zachary because he was a part of us. We got up "crying a river and slingin' snot," as my mother-in-law Tix would put it. And we felt not only a burden lifted, but a new sense of freedom.

Vickie tells the story of the first morning after everyone had left our home, after the funeral and all, and it was time to stumble our way into a very different future. She woke up and wondered how she was going to get out of bed. She felt someone in bed with her and there was that sweet curly-haired girl saying, "Mommy, I'm hungry." And as Vickie recounts, she said to herself, "Thank you, Lord, I need to get up." We were drawn into the future by grace and grace reminded us of life; it's just that it would be some time before we would catch up.

Hannah was born on August 4, 1986. That day had its own trauma. Vickie suffered with gestational diabetes for most of this pregnancy and Hannah weighed in at ten pounds at birth. Shortly after birth, various normal tests were taken, and the nurses removed Hannah to what we thought was the nursery. Once Vickie began recovering, I sought Hannah only to discover that she wasn't in the nursery. She had been moved to Neonatal Intensive Care, a surprise to both of us. With Nicholas at home enduring chemotherapy, this put me over the top. I pounded on the door hollering, "What the fuck are you doing with my daughter? What the hell is going on here? Will someone please tell me what's going on?" The doctor came to the door exhibiting a calm demeanor. "Look," I said, "I have a five-year-old son at home in chemo for leukemia and now our daughter is in intensive care with no one telling us what's going on. Why is she here? Why haven't you told us?" The doctor worked quickly to settle me down before explaining that Hannah struggled to process sugar and they were being cautious, believing nothing serious was amiss. All was well. Quite the day.

Hannah was baptized on October 12, 1986. Our church was meeting in the gym we had used for six years and a large crowd was expected. Family and friends from near and far joined us for a day of celebration in the midst of the trauma of Nick's chemotherapy. With many present, Hannah was baptized. We followed with a celebration at our home. All our family came and of course Nicholas was there. We ate and drank and

2. *Book of Common Prayer*, 456.

then the reality of our home life broke in unexpectedly. Nicholas began showing spots on his legs, back, and arms. This indicated a condition called petechiae, which required the transfusion of platelets in order to stop any bleeding. While celebrating with a couple of drinks, traveling to Children's Hospital wasn't tops on my list, but this was my call. My dad offered to come with me, and I said, "Dad, that's fine, but this probably will take three to five hours including lots of waiting." (My Dad's honest prayer would be "Grant me patience, Lord, but hurry.") Still, he wanted to come along. So his capacity for patience met his wall of tolerance and he spent a good deal of time walking around, occasionally coming back into the emergency room to watch football.

Nicholas was fine. This wasn't new to him. He was sad to miss "Sissy's party." Dad wondered, "Has this happened often?" I told him, "Yes, this or something similar happens all the time. We have developed our own routine about expected and unexpected issues. Sometimes I take Nicholas while Vickie sits with Hannah. Sometimes the opposite. We're trying to give our kids the best and soundest home we can. This is exhausting, Dad, but necessary." Dad said, "You and Vickie are doing a great job. I had no idea what treatment required from parents. Thanks for letting me come along."

Leaving Hannah's celebration broke my heart. For just a few moments that day all was well with our family. This would be one of several events altered in her life because of a brother with leukemia. Her name is no coincidence: she embodied our ongoing prayer request for grace.

Hannah means grace and she always has been grace in our lives, to this day. Dear Hannah, who spent five months with her grandparents in Arkansas while her brother and parents went through the transplant process. She became our lifeline. She demanded we pay attention to her and our hearts, my heart, continues to be deeply attached to her, unable to put into words my gratitude for the lifeline she demanded and provided and still does to this very day. And yet, all was not easy for this sibling of a brother who died.

A psychologist at the old Children's Memorial Hospital in Chicago said that Hannah wouldn't be troubled by this experience, as she wouldn't remember much. How mistaken she was. Nearly eighteen years later Hannah appeared on a panel of people who had experienced the death of a sibling. When it was her time to answer the first question she began answering and was soon overwhelmed with tears and obvious signs of grief. I wondered if we had missed with her. Had we ignored her? Assumed she was handling this on her own? Never seeking a chance for her to open up on her own experience? Beset by our own grief were we unable to reach out to her? Early on Vickie and I learned that doing our best to not have this experience dominate our parenting of Hannah and later Zachary became essential. We thought this was the thing to do. I can't help but think we somehow let Hannah down, however.

Vickie and I talked about Nicholas all the time but didn't necessarily talk directly to Hannah about her feelings. When her tears poured forth so many years later, I was struck by the intensity of her pain and loss and felt that we had overlooked the obvious. Perhaps we didn't want to burden her more. Perhaps we couldn't face such intimacy between ourselves. Perhaps we thought if we brought Nicholas up too much, she'd feel we didn't love her as much as her dearly departed brother. She was two-and-a-half when her brother died. We had her brought in to see his body, but she didn't attend his funeral. It all seemed right back then but not now. At the same time, we wanted to save her the pain, I guess. Or save us the pain?

Through it all, Hannah embraced life! When she was six she approached me knowing I had taken Nicholas to Disney World when he was about seven and asked, "Do I have to die for you to take me to Disney World, Dad?" The answer was no, so off we went when she was in kindergarten. We had the time of our lives. Later she was off on an airplane by herself at seven to visit a friend in Tennessee. While so much of Nicholas's life was accelerated due to illness and death, the challenge with Hannah was to support her life unfolding, as her life was to uniquely unfold.

Every stage of life brings mild aftershocks. When Hannah got married in 2012 in a beautiful service in our cathedral, I walked her down the aisle, her beauty inside and out, very aware that we were stepping into a new life surrounded by all the people who had helped us survive, heal, and grow. My heart could not contain the joy and love, nor could I find words for my gratitude for Vickie and for God and most especially for Hannah.

Zachary was born on January 29, 1991, not quite two years after Nicholas died. Vickie and I knew we wanted a third child and the circumstances of what occurred with Nicholas only reinforced the decision. We had interviewed a genetic specialist regarding childhood cancers, and he noted that there was nothing in Nicholas's genetics that would give cause to worry about another child. This news gave us additional confidence in having a third child. Along came Zachary.

When Nicholas and Hannah were conceived, the ability to determine the gender of the baby was clouded by fuzzy ultrasounds. Since Vickie was over thirty-five when Zachary was conceived, she required an amniocentesis. No simple process, a long needle was inserted into the sac with her bladder full to overflowing, and a bit of amniotic fluid was removed for exploration. When we returned a week or so later the doctor said all was well with the baby. The staff at the doctor's office kept asking if we wanted to know the sex of the baby. I said emphatically, "No!" The nurse offered to write down the sex on a piece of paper we could take along so if we wanted to know later, we could read the paper. That's what we did. We weren't one minute outside the door when I asked for the piece of paper and looked to discover we were having a boy. We both stopped and broke down and cried.

Rabbi Ed Friedman noted that whenever a child is born after the death of a sibling, the child is inevitably seen as a replacement and it requires great discipline to appreciate the new child's uniqueness.[3] When Zachary was baptized in 1991 a parishioner came up to me afterwards and said, "That was an incredible act of faith." I looked at her with confusion. "What do you mean" I asked. She responded, "Well, to have buried one of your children, to go ahead and have another, and to have him baptized after all you went through; that's a deep statement of faith." Perhaps we were acting our way into a new way of thinking? I don't know.

When Zachary was about one-and-a-half, he was playing with his friend Jessica in the backyard. A friend commented that he looked a lot like Nicholas from behind, and he did. Nick had good-sized ears like his father, grandfather, and great-grandfather on both sides of his family. Zachary also had the same ears. He suddenly turned around and I realized he wasn't Nicholas. Another aftershock of grief! Tears of grief overwhelmed my heart. Shortly I returned to the backyard with a heart filled with gratitude that Vickie, Hannah, and I would be blessed by Zachary (whom God remembers) and the joy of raising him with the joy of raising Hannah. He was a complete and separate human being all to himself.

All has not been perfect. We went through a period of time where Zach struggled with two realities. One was that he never knew his brother in the flesh. Secondly, this reality separated him from one significant family experience that all others had as a reference. We fulfilled our promise to Nicholas and introduced Nicholas's story to Zachary as Zach matured. As he gained more knowledge about that family experience from us and from

3. Friedman, *Generation*, 42.

others and from observing his parents in moments of overwhelming grief, he began to think we didn't love him as much as we loved Nicholas. I can still remember the conversation in his bedroom when I reassured him that we were so grateful he had been born; that I grieved that he didn't know his brother; that what he saw was his parents trying to move forward in our lives; that he, Zachary, was an incredible blessing to our family; that we loved him for the unique person he was and was becoming; that we were grateful beyond words that he was now in our family. His tears gently ended, and a smile returned, punctuated by getting on my lap and a warm hug.

Recently Zachary, now thirty, and I had a conversation about the effect of Nicholas's death on his life. He commented that Vickie and I were always there for him and he didn't feel slighted or pressure from us as the replacement. What he did say was interesting. "Dad, you and Mom did a great job with both Hannah and me. I don't know how you did it. What I miss is having an older brother. I miss having an older brother to learn from, play with, live with, and more. I don't miss him because I didn't know him. I miss what I think life would have been like with an older brother."

It took me a long time to discover the impact of Nicholas's death on my family. A wedge fell into family closeness; while grieving separately and reinventing our relationship, family was akin to a beautifully painted landscape. Everywhere you look on the finished canvas there is something new to see and perhaps to even notice for the first time. With the death of any loved one a place appears on the canvas that no longer takes paint. One can try and try and try but the landscape is changed. The open spot may be small or large. When my Grandfather Johnson died the spot taken from the landscape was microscopically small. When my son Nicholas died a significantly larger piece of the landscape lost color and wouldn't take paint again. Still doesn't take paint. Looking back, I realize family on both sides had no idea how to deal with Nicholas's dying nor with his grieving parents.

One day, while Nicholas was within three weeks of dying, my dad sat at the breakfast table lamenting how much pain this was causing my mother. I looked at him incredulously and said, "Are you kidding me? My son, your grandson, is in there dying and you're worried that this is tough on Mom? What about Nicholas? What about Vickie and me? Mom? Are you fucking kidding me?" After several moments of uncomfortable silence, I said, "Tomorrow morning you are to be here by 10 AM with your Prayer Book and you will lead prayers in his room, and you will lay your hands on him as his grandfather and bless him. And I don't want to hear about poor mom again." He grew quiet.

He showed up the next day with my mom. We all entered Nicholas's room and my dad drew out his worn 1928 Book of Common Prayer and said the prayers that meant a lot to him. He laid his hands on his head and blessed him. And we cried. And then we ate. I thanked my dad. He thanked me.

Vickie's family was different in their grief. Her parents were present and silent. They helped when needed and listened often. The coffee pot was always on and food readily available. They knew what a vigil was and coming from a life centered in family and patience, were able to sit and love without demands. When Nicholas finally died the pain was as overwhelming for them as for the rest of us. Memories of those days are cloudy at best.

I don't even recall the first time we went back to their home after Nicholas died. When they found out Vickie was pregnant again, they got scared and nervous about how all this would turn out. But they loved Zachary as they loved Hannah and as they had loved Nicholas. It makes me sad, even as I write this, to think of how heartbroken they were and the way the pain lived in their hearts and on their faces for the rest of their lives.

When Vickie and I went to clear out her family home after her dad died in 2009, we learned even more. Exploring the drawers in a house over forty years old is like an archaeological exploration, like a dig. As I reached deeper and deeper into the drawers, I quickly learned that history had been pushed to the back of the drawer. After pictures of Vickie's brother Steve, who had died three years before, we then came upon all the memorabilia of Nicholas, and each drawer was likened to a return in time to when he was alive. That approach worked for them; the further they pushed his pictures and gifts back into the drawer the less they were reminded on a daily basis of what they already knew to be true; Nick was dead, and their hearts were crushed.

Nicholas's spirit floated nearby whenever our families gathered. One year at Christmas Vickie had decided to have the first set of baby shoes bronzed for all three children. One of each pair was for us, and another was for her mom. When Tix opened the box, she put her hands down and said, "Oh Vickie!" She took out the first shoe and laughed. She took out the second shoe and laughed. Then she paused and looked around and looked at Vickie, her face asking the million-dollar question: was there a third shoe in the box for her dear Nicholas? The pause seemed to last forever. She reached into the box and wrapped her hand around the third shoe, shot up out of her chair, and walked quickly out of the room, crying. Vickie got up and went to her side. The tears were of love and gratitude.

One year the folks at St. Michael's, where I was serving, were getting a bit frustrated with me, believing I was stuck in grief and not able to move on and be helpful in the present. Once my resentment quieted down so I could hear, Art Kinney, a strong leader of the church and a personal mentor of mine, approached me and simply said, "Father, you got to move through this. No one expects you not to be sad at times, but life is moving on and people here are counting on you and they're not sure you can help them. And it's time for new sermon stories. Honestly, Father, people roll their eyes now when you bring up another story of Nicholas. It's been six years."

Again, I asked Dr. Ed Friedman in Maryland for help learning more about family emotional systems process. I got four minutes to seek his coaching. I told him what Art had said. Ed responded, "The answer is in your family. Go to your family and they will give you the answer." That was all he said. We walked for two more minutes in silence.

Two weeks later my dad and I were playing in a golf tournament in Florida at his country club. Taking the risk, I told Dad what the parish had said to me. He didn't get angry. I asked him how he dealt with Nicholas's death. He said, "Well, every morning I open the drawer on the side of my desk and there's his picture and I say, 'you little bugger.' Then I say a prayer giving him into God's hands for that day and close the drawer. I do that every day." My dad had given me all I needed for the next step in moving forward. From that day on I have given Nicholas into God's hands, every day, and thanked God for the gift of Nicholas. "A burden shared is a burden lifted."

All family members and friends each come to face this incredible word *never*. "Never say never!" I can't tell you how many times I've said that because, well, we just don't know, I don't know. But, in reality, I did know. In *Lament for a Son*, Nicholas Wolterstorff notes one of the single most substantial offerings to the awareness of grieving the death of a child, is the resignation to the reality of never.[4] "Never" won't be satisfied by an emotional wink or a nod. "Never" demands attention because if we stay sane, and that can be a big if, "never" brings into focus the permanence of the change that has happened and the continued changes that will unfold as time moves on. One significant change for all generations in a family is the

---

4. Wolterstorff, *Lament*, 15.

death of the vision of life that ended in the last breath of our child that died. The door mentioned in an early chapter fades from sight.

What a simple word really. *Never*. Bereaved families often celebrate the grace of living through the first-year anniversaries of everything related to their child who has died: first birthday, first holidays, first anniversary of death, and more. Friends and family actually congratulate us. As major psychological and emotional hurdles, these hurdles appear insurmountable as the particular day approaches. For me, momentary relief quickly gave way to despair, once again, as I began to understand that Nicholas would never be with us again in the flesh.

Meaningful holidays always accentuate the loss. When the extended family gathers everyone notices the empty places. I understood the empty places previously occupied by the elderly, but those, in some way, made sense. The spots left by children and those the same age as Vickie and me proved more obvious and therefore more painful to digest. Most people say that Christmas, or some other special day, is difficult. We hope to survive this first Christmas, Yom Kippur, Easter, birthdays, and so much more. Yet again I know that regardless of what I believe and think about forever, "never" is the honest truth about seeing and being with Nicholas again in this life. Planning activities helped for about three years and then compulsive planning gave way to celebration, reflection, and tears. But "never" is still "never"!

The landscape changes for everyone in the family. My niece Alexandra, who was Nicholas's age confidante as he approached his death and with whom he shared things that were sacred to the two of them, has a significant hole in her family landscape because of the closeness they shared. When her first son was born, she and her husband Dave named him Benjamin Nicholas as a sign of intentionally remembering him and the place he holds in her soul. Nine months older than Nicholas, she is acutely aware that she carries a double burden for her Aunt Vickie and Uncle Al and does so with love and generosity of spirit. She continuously integrates us into her family because she is loving and being loved by two families, her own and ours, in special ways.

Chapter 8

Companions

We need not walk alone.[1]

VICKIE AND I WERE invited to dinner with four other couples, all good friends, at one of their homes. This was our first time out after Nicholas got sick and we were ready for a night away. Our destination was less than a mile away and we had a competent babysitter with clear instructions on when to call us (no cellphones yet, landline only.) Early into the evening we received a call that Nicholas was throwing up. We immediately jumped into the car and sped home. He had the flu. Vickie and I decided she would stay home, and I would return to the dinner. When I arrived the dinner table that had ten chairs when we left was reduced to eight chairs. Living on the edge of life and death with Nicholas, this action frayed my already sensitive nerves. I turned around and left in tears, unable to process what I felt.

Companions fell into two timelines and two realities. Some companions were present as Nicholas received treatment and sought to live. Other companions entered our lives after he died. Some lived in both spaces. Some companions showed up in the flesh. Some companions can, and could only be, described as angels. What follows are six people who became deep companions.

The first person I'd like to include was introduced in an earlier chapter. He is Fr. Roy (aka Holy Joe) Hendricks. In January of 1988 after Nicholas relapsed and his chances for survival decreased substantially, I went to visit my bishop, Frank Griswold. I needed a companion to walk with me and thought he was the person. When I told Frank what had happened, and

1. The Compassionate Friends.

49

what lay ahead in the future, he noted that he wasn't particularly gifted with that kind of support, but he knew someone who was, Fr. Roy Hendricks. He made a call on my behalf and the following week Roy agreed to a visit.

Roy and his wife, Marian, lived north of Rockford, Illinois, at the Aldersgate Retirement Home (Methodist). Roy began ministry as a Methodist pastor and eventually moved to the Episcopal Church. He was a strong advocate for the poor and homeless and one who disregarded the foolishness of institutions, especially the local church, when neighborhoods called for outreach and service. Two congregations removed him from the pastorate due to his religious institutional disobedience. He and Frank Griswold crossed paths when both served in the Philadelphia area. Their ministries were moving in different directions. Frank referred me to Roy because he and Marian had lost a child, John, to Ewing's sarcoma in the 1950s.

Upon arrival at his room, Roy immediately gave me a lemon drop, invited me in, and offered for me to lay down for a few minutes to unwind from the drive. He stood about six feet two inches and carried a significant tire around his belly. His face reflected joy. His eyes were dark and penetrating. His right hand shook but not such that the shaking impeded actions. He had a crop of white hair tinted with a bit of black, parted on the left side. His face was always, over all the years I visited him, clean shaven. He walked slowly due mostly to his age and some arthritis. He had testicular cancer years before and had his testicles removed. I only know that because he shared that in a story about people drowning in self-pity for medical issues. He didn't tolerate self-pity. Roy enjoyed many activities at Aldersgate and created a few himself. When we later walked to lunch, clearly everyone knew him due to his willingness to be accessible. Yet I kept thinking of how he also didn't entertain fools. He was graceful to all and also careful with some.

As creative and institutionally disobedient as Roy was, Marian served as the keel of the boat of their lives. A small woman of about five feet four inches, she suffered from a rounded back and some serious arthritis. While Roy's grief packed seen and unseen levels of emotion, Marian lived by practicality. She lived with her hands in the dirt, gardening a large outdoor plot until they could not handle that physically and then she found her place in the greenhouse. She loved red geraniums.

They lived in different places of continuing grief over the loss of John. Marian only asked essential questions. Dark-trimmed glasses surrounded her penetrating eyes. She was also intolerant of self-pity and believed moving forward was critical to recovery. They had four children in total. They had no contact with their three living children, who were older than Vickie and me at the time. While details were unclear, the family had once had a serious falling-out around responses to John's death and the occasional angry and judgmental spirit of their father, Roy. One of their sons had a particular problem at the time with drugs. The two daughters simply needed space for their sanity. I finally met them at their parents' funerals.

A relationship with Roy was characterized by random and chaotic communication. He'd send a note with writing all over the envelope, with stamps inside or some saying, perhaps even a card to send back to him. He sent $2 bills to Nicholas, Hannah, and Zachary. In fact, he gave Nicholas enough bills that Nick signed each of them and gave them out to his family and friends as his estate. I carry one with me all the time. Roy was also notorious for the way he challenged thinking and believing. Until their health stopped them, Roy and Marian traveled every other year to Jamaica to lead a healing mission. They loved the people and the people loved them. He often asked me to go with him, and I regret that I never did. He often said that one has never experienced faith until one has worshipped with an African-based people. Many years later, on a trip to Sudan, I found this to be so true. And, funnily enough, in the African worship in Sudan, time made no difference.

Roy drew people to him. I certainly wasn't the only person entrusted to his care. People from his entire career and his new environment vied for time or a message from him. The phone rang all the time and he answered all the time. He called me "honey." I thought that strange at first but not later. Later I thought that an expression of his love. He never said goodbye on a phone conversation. He would just hang up.

Each visit to Aldersgate proved unique. One time he had invited another bereaved father who played the bagpipes. He insisted we go outside and parade around the home with the bagpipes playing away. I felt stupid and yet I went anyway. I simply trusted him such that his suggestions became pathways to strength, healing, and grace. Most visits we had lunch. We would walk down the line and he would load food onto my plate, and when we sat down, he would regale me with his brutal comments about other residents.

One day shortly after Nicholas died, I recall sitting on the cool tile floor in our master bathroom crying uncontrollably and feeling quite sorry for myself. I called Roy and we talked for some time. He sought to draw me out of the depression and grief, but I resisted. Finally, he said, "Honey, you make me sick! Get up! Shave your face! And then go help somebody!" He hung up on me. His bluntness in a spirit of love shook me out of my pity party and motivated me to get up and get out.

Then one day sometime in 1999, I came to take Roy and Marian out for dinner. They had a favorite Chinese restaurant in mind. So, we got in the car and headed out. I kept asking for directions and he kept giving them to me. My mental image of them was one of being in their right minds and aware of what was happening around them. However, when we passed the same Chinese restaurant twice and then on the third pass he said that was the one, I knew that one or both of them had begun the slow slide into dementia. We ate our dinner as I took charge in suggesting menu items. Then we went home and I walked them to their apartment heartbroken. But they had had a blast.

A couple of months later we planned another visit. When I arrived at their apartment something was different. Roy shared with me, through his tears, that Marian had been moved to the Alzheimer's rooms. Before lunch we walked down to her room. Roy, of course, knew everyone and his presence brought joy to so many people. We stepped into Marian's room and she was sitting in a chair by the window. She didn't recognize me, but she did recognize Roy. He reminded her several times of who I was and there seemed to be a glimmer of recognition, but not much, as she asked questions that six months ago she knew the answers to. I felt uncomfortable. My grandmother died of Alzheimer's but that had been nearly thirty years ago. Roy took the lead and we stayed and prayed and had lunch. And by now the tables had turned. I sought to be there for them as they had been there for me.

We visited about every two months and kept in touch by phone and cards, but nothing like before. Each visit he was heartbroken and yet fighting on to live life. Each visit, as he got older, he talked more and more about John. He finally shared that he didn't believe in heaven. Rarely swearing, he said that all this talk of heaven was a bunch of bullshit. "What?" I asked. "Oh honey, our dead are gone, and we will be too. Live now and surrender later." At the time this answer devastated me, probably because in the early stages of grief the notion of something to look forward to in terms of reunion with Nicholas seemed to placate the grief. I didn't ask Roy any questions about his answer. We had lunch and a lemon drop and a prayer of healing and I headed home.

I returned several weeks later. Roy was preparing to move from his apartment into a smaller room that he could manage by himself, leaving him more time to be with Marian. His tremors had intensified and his memory had become a bit shaky. We visited Marian and then went out for dinner at his favorite Italian restaurant. We ate to our stomachs' limit and returned to Aldersgate. We walked to his old apartment and hugged.

Then Marian died. One day she lived and the next day she died. Roy called and I reluctantly headed to Rockford. Her practicality informed her funeral plans. She went for immediate cremation and there would be no visitation of any kind. Frankly, there were no people to invite. The circle of us who attended the service, including their children, served as a circle of love, and the reception afterwards fit the simplicity of her desires. I returned home with Roy well in the company of his kids. A reconciliation had taken place when Marian began to live into Alzheimer's. Somehow this vulnerability broke down years of walls and the first signs of healing began to take place. They were grateful. They also noted to me that their dad, Roy, wasn't faring well either. I told them I'd keep in touch with him and them.

I honestly didn't handle Roy's death well. I think that's been true my entire life when it comes to men who were like a father to me, and Roy was certainly that. We had one last visit and this one challenged my own capacity for empathy and intimacy. He no longer wanted to leave Aldersgate for food, so we met in his apartment. He said the room pissed him off, so we headed to lunch at the usual dining room. After lunch we sat outside and then returned to his room. He took a seat on the bed and I on the chair opposite. "Honey, come over here and sit by me." I crossed the room and took a seat next to him on the twin bed. "Would you give me a hug?" Taken by surprise, I immediately turned towards him and placed my arms around him as he began to sob uncontrollably. "I haven't had anyone hug me in such a long time." Silence followed, except for the sound of weeping. I continued to hold him for some time, feeling awkward that the one who so often comforted me now asked comfort of me. Love freely given. After we both cried, I left for home, never to see Roy again.

Before Roy died, all of his family came to visit. They told me he was quiet but attentive. Soon after they left he died alone, as he had sensed most of his life to be alone but connected. Plans were practical. His body went for immediate cremation and the service was held in the local Methodist or Episcopal church. I can't remember, honestly. Further, I led the service and preached. His death left a deep hole in my soul. We had shared the unimaginable and helped each other, more him than me, find our way back to a different, yet no less satisfying, life.

Roy's ashes were taken to New England where the family, when the time was right, would bury them beside Marian's and John's. We were going to connect about that, with the loose lips of promises of attending, which never turned into action. The death of children teaches many things including what or who to hold on to, and whom to let go. I held on desperately to Roy because Roy gave me hope by his very existence.

I don't know how well or poorly I handle grief. I don't recall moments of profound sadness or tears, but I bet they took place. Losing anyone in relationship is traumatic and his death was no less so. I have five legacies from Roy. His legacies fill me with gratitude. The first of the day was learning what being a parish priest means. When he left our house before Nicholas died he blessed our house and said to me, "Don't ever leave a person's house without offering to bless their residence." After that, I never did, even if I didn't know the people very well.

The second legacy was the importance of acting one's way into a new way of thinking versus thinking one's way to a new way of acting. He believed in action as a component of grief healing. His prodding led me to remove items from Nick's room, return some to school, give his clothes away except for a few keepsakes, and bury his ashes quickly. Vickie and I did all of these.

The third legacy, and perhaps most important of all, was the lesson of silence in the face of conflict. I called once about an issue at St. Michael's, ranting and raving and asking his advice of what to do. He said, "Be quiet, honey, be quiet. If you're quiet you will learn all you need to know in a very short time. The information will simply come to you." His counsel on this one has proven to be helpful time and time again, right up to the present. Silence is where opportunity, God, and life intersect.

The fourth legacy was his courage. There was no experience of human life and death Roy would not willingly enter into for love. His Jesus was practical and helpful. That courage inspired the same courage in me and in parish ministry.

Finally, the fifth legacy taught me to avoid lingering in self-pity too long or I will become someone no one wishes to be with or talk to. He was impatient with my self-pity and, as noted earlier, pushed me to reach out, inviting my pain to be transfigured by the pain of others.

From my first contact by phone after the referral from Frank Griswold through daily ministry, which brings his memory to life, Roy has proven to be one of two companions through grief who became life companions through friendship. People like Roy come into our lives for a reason and for a period of time, and then they move on. This is not meant to be self-centered; we also enter and leave people's lives the same way.

Once Nicholas died, here came Mary Ann, companion number three (counting Marian as well as Roy). Mary Ann was an angel in disguise. She lived down the street from us. She had two daughters both older than our daughter Hannah. Before Nicholas died, we didn't know her very well. How does it happen that along whichever road we travel the divine Spirit seems to send us the right people at the right time to aid us on our way? And often these people turn out to be ones we don't know well or ones we never thought had it within them to help. They simply show up and without the need of any explanation pitch in and help. Mary Ann became a quiet angel.

The day after Nicholas died, she showed up at our home, walked in the door, and went to work; for many days after she continued to be present. She never asked to come over. Weeks after the funeral Mary Ann would come by, sweep up Hannah in her arms, and take her for a day of fun with her girls. The space was helpful. There are so many things to take care of after a death and very little energy to accomplish them. And Mary Ann helped give our daughter some joy and laughter. Vickie and I weren't the best people to bring forth those opportunities with a joyful spirit. We could "do" things but while the body was able, the spirit was weak. Hannah was our draw back into life. We became friends with Mary Ann and her husband, Keith. She was an active and gentle soul who continuously made herself available, especially to Vickie. She and Keith asked nothing of us and gave all the love they could.

Some people are focused on being and some on doing. Doing helped us as it does other bereaved parents. Many say that they will call or to call them if we need anything. That rarely happens. You see, what most people don't know is that bereaved parents have no energy to instigate anything. Faith reduces to the simple act of getting out of bed and trying to move forward. When Mary Ann embraced the "doing" of life, Vickie and I were free to move through the "being" of grief.

She had a hop to her step and a smile on her face. She entered our house full of energy and intuitively knew what to do, from sitting and listening to cleaning the bathroom. Standing nearly six feet tall, she had brown hair cut in a bobby-like look, brown eyes, and was thin as a rail. She was life incarnate and a wonderful antidote to grief. I'd come home from work and there she was talking with Vickie over coffee in our kitchen. We'd be sitting in our family room and one of her daughters would come calling for Hannah and off they would go laughing and excited.

Mary Ann lived the admonition "Faith without works is dead." This was not conscious on her part. Her ability to serve us in this way was unconscious and gracious. She never waited to be asked. She had courage. While she never talked about her faith or said, "I do this because of Jesus," the message she preached by the way she lived her life always pointed to something beyond herself. We needed both her actions and her faith, and she generously gave both.

Over time our friendship as couples grew. They provided what would become a necessity, a safe "place" to be, with no acting required. As the crowd diminished after Nicholas's funeral, Mary Ann kept the faith while others, and rightfully so, moved on with their lives. We were far behind, and with people like Mary Ann and Keith we didn't have to press to catch up with the world. Eventually they moved to Michigan and bought a deli and our lives drifted apart. Many years later we heard Keith had died from a stroke. People enter our lives for a time and a purpose. No reciprocity required. Pure gift!

All along the way were Hal and Linda Toberman, companions four and five. Sometimes companions in dying become companions in rising. That was true with Hal and Linda. In starting the church in Bloomingdale, I made 1,000 cold calls to families and one joined, the Tobermans. Like Mary Ann, Linda and Hal simply showed up.

On the night Nicholas died, as noted earlier, Linda and Hal showed up with John and Christine soon after the death. They offered an open presence. They offered no superfluous idioms or trite phrases of condolence. They asked if we needed anything but mostly sat around the table as the vigil unfolded and loved on Vickie, Hannah, Vickie's parents, Nicholas, and me. Their presence did not feel presumptuous due to the church connection.

Their children were very much the same way, often accompanying Hannah and Nicholas at our home. The Tobermans' son John was a particular friend of Nick's and stayed in touch with him to the end. As time wore on after Nick's death their daughter Christine became integral to our small community of people who joined us in remembering Nicholas, always on March 18 (the day he died) and August 1 (his birthday).

I'll never forget one March 18 when Nicholas was still buried at St. David's in Glenview (we later moved his ashes to St. Michael's in Barrington for proximity and to provide burial niches for Vickie and me) and we went to visit. We brought our Reese's Cups (Nicholas's favorite) and shed many a tear. We felt so terribly alone when, out of nowhere, there was this voice on the other side of the hedge, and it was Christine. We cried and cried and rejoiced in Christine's love. We went out for dinner, a Nick day tradition, and went home feeling deeply loved by God and Christine. Salving the wounds of grief doesn't take much. Mostly the salving takes friends realizing that, even years after the death, the bereaved parents may have difficulty for moments on such anniversaries and remembering, though often painful, remains deeply appreciated.

Hal and Linda were beautiful angels. On the second anniversary of Nick's death we planned some great extravaganza to avoid the pain and the Tobermans came along with us. That was the day when it became clear to Vickie and me that we didn't need compulsive plans for the entire day; we could spend some time alone and enjoy memories and even tears. This was a crucial turning point. Getting to that turning point was the direct gift of the love and friendship of Hal and Linda. Linda in particular became a listener for Vickie and a gentle hug of acceptance. Our families remain connected to this day.

And now, person number six. Many experiences describe a best friend forever. Bob Myers was and is that. I don't know where we met for lunch on that particular day. When we sat down and ordered the story unfolded. "Bob, this past week I took Nicholas to the clinic at Children's. A spinal tap took place in order to infuse a chemical called methotrexate directly into his spinal column." I was now talking through tears. "First, I had to chase him throughout the clinic because he knew what was next. He was crying and finally I cornered him and picked him up to take him into the back room, with a mixture of conviction and sadness. He finally goes completely limp and I place him on the table where he is placed in the fetal position." The crying prevented me from continuing for a moment. "So I hold him down . . . and he's so scared he shits on the table. 'Come on buddy, come on buddy . . . you're almost there . . .' I encourage him through nearly debilitating sadness and tears. Then the procedure is over, and he literally jumps off the table and is ready for all the treats he was promised before the procedure. And that's great. But, Bob, I'm a wreck. I can't believe that I had to hold him down like that so others could hopefully provide a cure. When

I studied about laying on of hands, I never thought this would be a means of laying on of hands for healing. Never." Then there was silence, my head down and shaking, tears. Bob sat in quiet. Slowly I raised my head, tears still streaming down my face. He came over and gave me a hug and then returned to his seat.

Quite often we hurt those we love the most. One day after Nicholas died, Bob and I stood outside Holy Comforter Episcopal Church in Kenilworth, smoking cigars and talking. We had just had lunch and all of a sudden I took off after him emotionally, claiming he wasn't there when I needed him. "Where were you? Where were you? You're supposed to be my best friend! Where were you?" The anger turned to tears and I collapsed into grief right there on the porch. Bob said, "I was there, and I'll be there now and always. I love you and nothing you can do can change that, my friend. My heart ached and aches for you."

Bob was a fellow Episcopal priest, and we first met in 1976 when Effie Kenyon from Seabury-Western Theological Seminary invited us with our spouses for brunch. We enjoyed many Bloody Marys and then headed to Hackney's on Harms Road for dinner with our wives, where we feasted on juicy burgers with all the works and incredible onion rings . . . and a few more drinks. The four of us soon became the best of friends, and eventually Bob and I became truly best friends.

Dr. Carl Christiansen once noted, and I paraphrase, "If we find one or two friends to travel with through life we are blessed." Bob became one of those friends and still is today. As couples we rotated having dinner and talking about everything we could imagine. We laughed mostly then. The tears would follow. Bob and I began a tradition that still exists to this day, of having lunch every month or so. Over time we became each other's confidants. He doesn't have pictures, but he sure has a mind full of stories. He taught me vulnerability, and more about love.

Bob earned his PhD in pastoral psychology and remained an assistant at the church in Kenilworth. I became an assistant in Glenview, a mere ten miles away. Then, Vickie got pregnant and Nicholas was born. And then Bonnie got pregnant and twins Mark and Andrew were born, both especially premature. Mark was basically fine. Andrew had significant issues. Both boys stayed in the Neonatal Intensive Care Unit for several months. When they arrived home, Mark was progressing well. Andrew had several challenges. For starters, he was deaf and partially blind. Further, his mental development was impaired and would be for the rest of his life. Identical twins with very different life circumstances. Our images of retirement became very different, as did our lives and marriages. Bob and I had envisioned retirement life with our spouses, healthy children, rocking chairs, whiskey, and cigars. We both learned a good deal about sorrow. Not that we needed more to bring us closer together in friendship, but sorrow did that and more.

Bob proved to be an invaluable companion on the journey of grief. The birth of his twins, the discovery that Andrew had issues, the death of his wife Bonnie, his leaving his parish church; all of that and more and few tears. Then the coronavirus appeared, and Bob faced the choice of keeping Andrew (then thirty-five years old) or returning him to Misericordia (a home for differently abled persons) where he would live for two months with no outside contacts, including his father. For the well-being of Andrew, Bob painfully elected to leave him in the care of his home at Misericordia. The first time Bob and Andrew Skyped Bob called me in tears. Andrew, while deaf, mute, and with the emotional level of a five-year-old, nevertheless could use sign language, about 500 signs. He kept signing his father through tears, "When are you going to come see me? When? When?" Bob was heartbroken that he could not, in Andrew's best interest, see his son, take him out for dinner at their favorite places, get Starbucks hot chocolate, and visit Walgreens for bright toys. My dearest and best friend experienced deep pain, and so did Andrew.

Bob taught me, and still teaches me, about love. No matter the fracas or situation I might experience or get myself into, he always reminded me that no matter what, he loved me. For one blessed with the wounds of my heart, this love, like that of Vickie, carried an immeasurable value. Built into this friendship of love was space for closeness and distance; for confusion and understanding; for anger and for joy; for sorrow and for redemption; for despair and hope. Dr. Christiansen was accurate!

Chapter 9

The Local Church

The local church is the hope of the world.[1]

BISHOP JAMES MONTGOMERY GAVE me the assignment to head to the Bloomingdale area in 1981 and start a church. Vickie, Nicholas, and I moved to the area and began working towards birthing a new community. The church began in people's living rooms, park picnic shelters, and eventually came to settle in the local grade school for the foreseeable future. The congregation was made up of a hodgepodge of people seeking a relationship with God for a variety of reasons.

We started with an average of sixty people in worship and eventually grew to over 150. In the Episcopal system, at the time, this was considered a great success. And yet the voice of evangelical Christianity was suggesting that any church under 200 in attendance could not remain self-sufficient. Success in one system was treading water in another. My mind knew Fuller Theological Seminary's assertion about church growth was accurate. Yet our system thrived on the English vicar model, which focused on caring for and being with people more than just reaching out to those who were hurting and seeking people.

Eventually our church purchased a three-acre piece of land on Army Trail Road, bordering a subdivision of "our kind of people." That meant well-to-do financially. With diocesan funding we bought the land, which included a house. We moved the church office to the house and began moving towards the idea of breaking ground for our own building. We paid no attention to the massive strip mall development on the other side of the

1. Anonymous.

street. Such blindness eventually reduced the potential effectiveness of the new church.

In 1987 construction began on the church building and over the next nine months the building for the Church of the Incarnation began to take shape. The diocese was so excited that they agreed to cosign on a loan that was substantial but affordable for the time. And, as noted earlier, we entered the building and began worshipping in the summer of 1988.

I have no idea what the congregation thought when Nicholas got sick in 1986. Vickie said, "They were shocked, devastated, sad, and horrified." Nicholas was only two months old when we arrived. While Vickie raised Nicholas, I raised a church. Seriously! I know people were sympathetic and willing to support us in any way we needed. I just don't recall what that support looked like.

We had been together as a church long enough to have significant conflicts about growing and adding new people. In the summer of 1987, the parish granted me more vacation time in lieu of an increase in pay, and my family and I were able to travel to Mackinac Island for five wonderful weeks. Nicholas was well and able to enjoy himself. We worried a bit about needing to bring him back to Chicago, but all went well . . . and then relapse and death.

How was I to access any hope when upon my return to active ministry my mantra was, "fake it till you make it"? Now I realize the church was doing the same thing. I no more knew how to pastor after such an experience than they knew how to pastor me. We were stuck, and no one thought to invite someone in to help us process what had taken place; we stumbled along directionless. I was selfish and wanted pain relief. I had no idea, nor did I really care, what the church thought. I looked out upon the congregation with little sympathy. I had nothing to give, and they still had needs and appropriately so. Additionally, how to connect our collective despair to the hope of Jesus was nonexistent.

The Sunday following Nicholas's funeral was Easter Sunday. I preached at our local church that had only recently opened. I hid blue balloons under the pulpit and let them go as a sign of hope. After all, the day was Easter, the feast of the resurrection. Without question that was the most willful sermon I had ever preached. Our bishop offered for me to use a supply person, but I thought being there would be better than being at home. I don't remember much about that Sunday or the ones that soon followed.

Two weeks after Nicholas died a parishioner came to see me. She was reaching out to me, but I had no space to help her with her grief. She came in and offered how sad she was for what had happened. She went on to tell me about how her dog had died, implying she knew what I was experiencing. On the outside I looked at her with the gaze of an experienced parish priest. On the inside I had to fight every inclination to blow this person out of the water with both the anger of grief but also the incredibility of her words. Within a few minutes I calmly ended the conversation and sat in my office wondering what to make of this. My heart was crushed, and my anger was piqued. She didn't know what she was saying. She hoped to form that deep connection with her parish priest. Like many, she wanted me to help her understand what had happened to my family. She was looking for reassurance that such an experience would not come to her family.

Three months after Nicholas died another parishioner came in for a conversation. He offered words of empathy for our experience but wanted to know when the church and I would get back to normal. From my desire to please I acted as if I knew what he meant and that, of course, we could find that old place again. Reassured, he left the office confident that the normal known months ago, before Nicholas's death, would return. That normal never returned again. That normal was based on all previous participants alive. Clearly that wasn't possible for me. I had no idea what any new normal looked like.

About four months after Nicholas died another parishioner approached me about having lunch. We met at a local eatery and talked. A week before my dad and I had met at the same place, when my dad suggested I might think of moving in hopes that a fresh start that would help us with the loss and pain. He had wisdom and love. This person from church suggested the same thing. I was offended by his suggestion but managed to keep my balance enough to ask him why. He went on to tell a heartbreaking story.

"There was this priest, Fr. Jackson, who also happened to be a friend of my dad's. Well, one day early in his ministry he accidentally ran over a three-year-old girl in the neighborhood of his parish and killed her. People were forgiving and understanding, and the family of the little girl also forgave him. The problem was Fr. Jackson could not forgive himself; nor would he seek help. He stayed in that same congregation for over thirty more years and watched as the congregation declined to the point where he barely received a salary. His family was nearly destroyed. He started drinking. No manner of reason permeated his belief that he was responsible, unforgivable, and with no way to carry this experience forward. His family resented him for staying. Children who left home did not return after leaving for college. He was a deep friend of my dad's and my dad often suggested he move, but Fr. Jackson could not bring himself to act. He needed to move and didn't and as a result he not only brought the family down, but the church also. That's why you need to move."

I sat stunned, small tears running down my face from the corner of my eyes. Lunch continued on a civil basis with talk about many things. When we parted I took his message to heart. Combined with the suggestion from my dad and the soon-to-be-explored ministry at a new church, God was at least asking me, asking us, to explore moving. Vickie and I talked in earnest about the question: Would we be able to move on from this loss if we continued to look at the circumstances surrounding his death on a daily basis? We concluded no. I had redecorated Nicholas's room, hoping to make the space into an office/guest room. It didn't work. We only spent time in that room when we wanted to recall his life and death, and pain became a quick companion. Time to move on.

Yet, this experience troubled before it was gone. This was true not only in the church, but also in my family and personal life. I could never be the priest and pastor I was before. Within four months, a friend approached me about moving to another church. I knew the "rules" that one doesn't move within a year of loss, but Vickie and I were ready to move on, believing that recovery would be difficult where we lived. Hannah was a different story. She loved our home in Bloomingdale and wanted to stay. For months after we moved to Barrington she kept asking when we were going to return to our "home." Friends leave her; brother leaves her; neighborhood leaves her; safe home leaves her. She became the epitome of resilience and grieving in more ways than simply losing her brother.

When we finally moved in June of 1990, just as the last boxes were being put in my car for the journey north, a woman driving by stopped her car, got out, gave me a hug, and said, "We're all sad to see you move, to go, but we understand; we all understand." She was a stranger. Intense focus on our own home and family made me blind to how Nicholas's life had affected others. I got in my car and cried the entire way to Barrington. Sometimes doing the right thing hurts so much worse than staying in place. What were we doing? Why were we moving? Vickie was even pregnant with our third child. We feared staying in that pain for the rest of our lives. We moved into the rectory (parsonage) in Barrington, located across from the local cemetery. Somehow we hoped that healing included ways to embrace "never."

Ah, the cemetery, Evergreen Cemetery. For two years that was the only place I ever walked or ran; I was comfortable with the dead. Within a month I knew where every child under twenty-one was buried and soon learned of the baby section tucked back in the southwest corner of Evergreen Cemetery. The names escape me now. Lap after lap after lap around the cemetery was spent seeking to calm the inner turmoil and find some relief from the pain. The prospect of living with the pain of grief for the rest of my life led me to believe that those below ground had it easier than those of us above ground. And then one day, while running back and forth in the cemetery, the Spirit spoke and I left the cemetery only to return occasionally when duty called, or simply to remember.

Demands of this new church in Barrington, much larger than the last one, required large amounts of time. Vickie and I were fine with that for the meantime. No matter how busy I was, once I was home the waves of grief returned. St. Michael's was patient and wanted to hear the story. Telling the story in any form is healing. I had another mission also—find any parents who had lost a child. I looked at all the plaques in the outdoor columbarium and quickly learned of two young people who had died. Their names were Paul and Nathan. In the midst of parish life, finding their parents became objective number one.

Nathan's parents lived two blocks from the church. In 1990 the culture still permitted unannounced visits on parishioners and so I walked to their home and introduced myself. They greeted me warmly and invited me in. As the time was later in the afternoon, they offered me a cocktail and I said yes. They refilled their glasses and we sat to visit. The first hour was spent in becoming familiar. My pastoral training taught the importance of allowing parishioners to bring up the topics on their minds and hearts. For some reason bringing up Nathan didn't seem the pastoral action to take, so I didn't. However, Nathan's mother, Barb, spewed forth about the death of their son Nathan, also from leukemia. From a combination of tears, and profound sadness, she told bits and pieces of the story.

The leukemia came upon him right after he turned four. Treatment was more barbaric then (the 1950s), and as she recalled this her tears turned into uncontrollable sobs. Nelson, the father of Nathan, sat with a smile on his face, fighting his urge to stop the conversation before he succumbed to the sadness. Slowly the rest of the story unfolded. Nathan made remission for a short period of time and then the disease returned, and he died at Children's Hospital in Chicago.

As we sat, tears subsided, and silence enveloped the space in their living room. I didn't know what to do or to say. Barb said, "I haven't talked about our beautiful boy for a long time. Always the tears." I responded, "Thank you for sharing all this about your life. Thank you. Thank you. I don't know what to say. Telling this is a gift that will help with the grief from the death of our son Nicholas." She said, "We knew you had lost a child and thought eventually you'd come over and we'd talk. Going to those places inside holds so much sadness and sorrow. We've tried to make the best of our lives and put the experience behind us, but that has continuously proved difficult to do. So maybe you can help us, and we help you?" I said, "I'd be grateful for that."

The following Sunday they were in church. They were sheepish towards me and I chalked that up to the raw vulnerability of our visit the previous week. We would visit many times over the ensuing years, until Barb died and Nelson moved to be closer to his surviving children. How does one ever repay a couple for their willingness to invite us into the depth of their loss? Not possible really, except, perhaps, to learn that our stories in time might help others heal.

Paul was sixteen and died from a car crash. Finding someone from his family to visit was difficult. The Frost family lived a good distance from St. Michael's, but eventually I found Paul's mom, Mary, home. She reluctantly invited me into her house (another cold call), knowing right away why I was there. After she offered something to drink, we sat down in their living room.

She said, "I heard about your son. Heartbreaking. What happened?" I proceeded to tell her the condensed story. "Well, at least our son wasn't so young, and we got a bit more time with our Paul." I ignored her attempt at pain competition and asked, "What happened? If you don't mind sharing what took place?" Tears began to line her face and she put her head down and wrung her hands. All of a sudden the darkness of the room made sense. We sat in silence for what seemed like an eternity. I was wondering if I had done the right thing in coming to visit her.

"Well, Paul had just received his license. He was like all of sixteen years old, eager to drive and willing to run any errand that would give him more time behind the wheel. I don't even remember what he went to buy. What I recall is hearing the ambulances and thinking, 'I hope that's not my son.'

Shortly after, the Lake County Sheriff entered our driveway and immediately I knew my premonition was true; our Paul was either hurt or had died in whatever accident those ambulances were addressing. The officers approached the door and I remember answering in a complete fog."

The sheriff informed her of Paul's serious accident and told her, "He was taken immediately to Good Shepherd Hospital and we are uncertain of his condition."

Mary said, "Well, I called my husband at work downtown and got in my car and headed to the hospital, hoping beyond hope that he was still alive. When I entered the ER all the staff had their heads down and would not make eye contact with me. Fear rose as bile in my throat. 'Where's my son? Is he alive?' A doctor quickly stepped in front of me and took me by the arm and moved us to a place where we could talk.' 'I'm sorry but your son didn't make it. The complications from the accident; we simply couldn't save his life. I'm so sorry.'"

She continued, "I was numb. Those words could not cross my mind. Impossible. I first thought that I needed to call my husband but then I was overcome with the need to see Paul so I chased the doctor down and asked, 'Can I see him?' He said, 'Let me check. Why don't you stay right here, and I'll have a nurse come and get you.'"

"After what seemed like forever, this older nurse with a neutral look on her face came and took me by the arm and led me behind the ER curtain and there he was, my dear Paul, covered by a blanket except for his head. His face was lacerated and covered with bruises. I fell apart, engulfed in sadness the likes of which I had never felt before this time. After a few minutes I looked around the room and noticed all sorts of medical stuff indicating all they had tried to do to save his life. Later I learned that he was dead when he arrived, but they always try. My dear son."

"I called my husband at work and told him that Paul had died in a car wreck. I heard him howl with pain. A coworker picked up the phone and I told him what had happened. The friend brought my husband to the hospital. In the meantime, I also called our priest and he arrived within ten minutes."

Mary's husband would never see me. He was angry with God and blamed God for Paul's death. But when her husband was near death from cancer, he called me to visit. He wondered if God would take him home to see Paul even if he was so angry. I confidently replied, "Oh yes, God's been waiting to bring you home for years. And Paul? Well, he's there at the gate, ready."

Mary and I grew to become friends and stayed in touch after she moved to the Southwest to be near her daughter. She opened up into the beauty of life and into the depth of the spirit at work in the desert. Slowly we drifted apart and then I had word she died. She proved to be one of the most helpful and wonderful people while I was at St. Michael's.

The brokenness of the parish and the brokenness of my heart opened a place to grieve through preaching. They tolerated my need to tell parts of the story over and over again. People said, "How did you do that? I don't think I could ever recover if one of my children died." I responded every time with nothing but gratitude and appreciation for the love of these people. And yet too much of a good thing is still too much.

I retired from St. Michael's on December 31, 2010. In January the parish held a roast and we laughed and cried. I was able to tell them then and at worship the next day, my last Sunday, how grateful I was for their love, grace, and tolerance. While I helped bring the church back to health, they helped bring my family and me back to health. No words existed to capture the depth of love and gratitude. So I simply said, "Thank you."

Chapter 10

Culture, Expectations, and Grief

Culture refers to the made and intended world.
It is a world of values, because people make and do things
for a purpose and design them to serve a good—in most cases
a human good.[1]

RANDY LEWIS WAS A senior executive with Walgreens. He and his wife's second child, Austin, have autism. Randy used his influence with Walgreens to employ over 1,000 people with disabilities in its distribution centers. Since this initiative within a major business culture drew from Randy's Christian faith, I asked him to preach one Sunday and tell his story. This was his opening line: "One thing I have learned is that all of us parents of children with disabilities share the same prayer: to live one day longer than our child." After pausing to let that sink in, he continued, "Because we know what's waiting for them. Who will care for and protect them after we are gone? Who will love them? In a world of limited resources, who can save enough to set aside the money needed? Who has other children who are able and willing to take this all on?"[2]

While feigning continued interest I began to process this insight. My godson Andrew was quite differently abled, and I immediately wondered if this was true of Andrew's dad, my best friend, Bob? Randy's opening comment further informed the notion that pain is real and relative.

I wondered how does the pain of living with a disabled child who is dependent on others for basic needs and the worry of leaving them

1. Wells, *Future*, 117.

2. Lewis, *Goodness*.

68

compare to the death of a child? I knew some parents of children with cancer continuously had their children treated in order for them to stay alive, regardless of the child's wishes or the level of suffering. What could be worse than losing a child? As Randy talked my understanding of pain stretched once again.

Competition and comparison! Pain speaks to pain without any filters. Pain doesn't judge pain. Pain seeks recognition and eventually healing. Pain leaves scars. Pain changes us, particularly pain that emanates from that "broken-openedness" place within. All humanity shares pain. All of us! No exceptions! And pain changes the trajectory of life.

There is a cultural norm that states the death of a child is the worst pain a person could ever experience, as if some competition or spreadsheet exists measuring different levels of pain as determined by the source of pain. There are cultural expectations about how long grief takes and specific guidelines or stages one "should" follow. These are also used to determine whether or not the person is healing. No matter what the experts say, as each of us live in our suffering the pain is most significant to us. Is there more comfort between the possibility of leaving a differently abled child than in the death of a child or in a dad who, by divorce decree, can never see his kids? Which hurts the most?

Early on I drank the coffee that said the death of a child was worse than anything else. At the same time, I started listening. Near 9/11 in 2002 a firefighter from Engine Company 55 in New York came to our church to tell the story of that day one year ago. His name is John Olivero. We were also interested in how he looked at his faith as the year had unfolded. As the story began he was resolute and confident, until he came to the part where he began to mention the five firefighters from Engine 55 who died that day. In particular he mentioned one firefighter who had climbed up tower one. Many others did also, but in this case his parents, living across the Hudson in clear view of the towers, knew he was in tower one. They were praying for his safety. Moments later they watched the tower fall and knew their son had died. In recounting this, John began to cry, the church was silent, the pain nearly overwhelming. Stunned by the depth of these losses, the congregation sat in silence. I went up and put my arm around John, asking if he wanted to continue. He did. That was one of the best Sundays ever at St. Michael's. Nine hundred people sitting quietly in the suffering of another human being. So, whose pain was worse?

Our culture is awkward when it comes to dealing with death in general and particularly awkward in working with bereaved parents. What was such an easy question in 1985, "How many children do you have?" became a more difficult question for us to answer after 1989. That one was particularly awkward because for many years answering "two children" (Hannah and Zachary) made me feel as if I was ignoring or forgetting Nicholas. Not rational, but true. On the other hand, answering "three with one in heaven" presented another challenge of wandering into the story of what took place and the fear of feelings erupting anywhere and anytime. And the exhaustion of telling the story.

One challenge regarding grief focused on the word *success*. Soon after Nicholas died, Vickie and I attended a Compassionate Friends meeting. Compassionate Friends began because a chaplain in England noticed that one bereaved family was able to help another bereaved family better than he could. The organization of providing those peer situations took the form of chapters of Compassionate Friends around America and eventually in many places in the world. For years Vickie and I found comfort with our once-a-month Friday night meeting. We received inspiration, education, comfort, and hope from these gatherings. One couldn't help but notice that there were new people at every meeting and the stories and emotional expressions of these folks kept our broken hearts wide open.

One leader used to say, as he was leaving, "It does get better!" For years I wanted to strangle him, as there was no clear pathway to "better." A dear man named Foster Roser, who had been coming for over six years, mentored us. That seemed like an eternity. Now that time seems like a drop in the bucket. He was kind, accepting, and very tolerant. He exuded patience and wisdom with newcomers that insured many of us would come back. He offered no easy steps towards healing. He simply lived the mantra of Compassionate Friends, "We need not walk alone."

My heart broke when he announced that he was leaving the group after one more meeting. After seven years he believed the time was right to move into another direction of helping people. Vickie and I actually led our group for eighteen months and volunteered for various labors of love in support of meetings and people. We laughed and cried together and healing gradually took place. The Compassionate Friends came to life.

Years later, Compassionate Friends spent months toying with a vision like "the successful resolution of grief." We were captured by a cultural norm expectation. I knew in the moment that goal would probably prove unreachable, as that idea unconsciously suggested that at the base all people grieve the death of our children in the same way and with the same objective. Not true! Quick to add to this goal of resolution came the thought that only one path will take me to that place. The idea of grief set free ultimately moved me in the opposite direction.

I also personally know the origin of the use of that word *resolution*. Like all bereaved parents I get tired of the pain and hope that at some point in the future the pain will simply go away—be resolved. Who wouldn't? You choose. Move through a day carefree, or sit in the corner of the bathroom crying hysterically as your heart breaks in two? Eventually for me "resolution" was impossible. I looked another way to learn how to sit in grief. Words like *resolution* proved dangerous and inevitably provided a means of "measuring up" that led to more pain; this time of guilt and shame much like the object relations class I took in seminary that taught about how we attach to others and how we separate, especially in death. Here was where the expectations, that one "should" be well on one's way to recovery or resolution by the one-year anniversary of the person's death, were formed.

Our culture constantly searches for simplified ways to process pain in grief. Insights in the grief process followed the publication of Elisabeth Kubler-Ross's seminal work[3] in which she outlined the five stages of grief a person experienced emotionally as their life was ebbing away. This cutting-edge work quickly became the norm for exploring the process of grief following death, as much or more than within the process of dying (probably because we search for ways to feign control over erratic emotional and spiritual experiences). Kubler-Ross's work became one of the first to explore and accept the reality of death in the medical world. She developed five stages of grief: denial, anger, bargaining, depression, and acceptance.

The culture of working with the bereaved quickly embraced this study and once again believed that her work described a step-by-step process, this time insuring a certain outcome embraced by the word *acceptance*. Bereaved parents began to measure their process through these five stages, generally acting as if each phase had to be completed before moving on to the next stage. That was never Dr. Kubler-Ross's desire or her research goal. But once again our desire to pursue the hope of a less painful recovery process encouraged bereaved parents in particular to attempt to move quickly through the stages.

3. Kubler-Ross, *On Death*, 37–132.

Over time we began to see that her work represents phases versus stages and that often the phases overlap. What happens when a person, believing that once a stage is complete and they move on to the next stage, suddenly finds themselves back in a previous stage? This person, who is grieving the loss of a loved one, might think something is wrong with them as they are not able to remain at the "stage" they had reached. The softening from stages to phases helped people understand that grieving isn't an easily measured process with a guaranteed outcome, especially in the case of the death of children. The softening from stages to phases helped me.

Bereaved parents could see signs of themselves in more than one or all of the phases at one time. If they experience anger while feeling depressed about the overwhelming feelings of grief, it doesn't mean failure. Such experiences pointed out that people move around and between phases with ease, depending on life's particular circumstances. What became apparent to those of us grieving, and those studying those of us grieving, was that more than a process, grief is an experience of loss that we struggled to embrace in our consciousness as well as in our lives. The phases became guideposts to help in determining where we are in the process at any given time. The doors of the cultural prison were gradually opening. The last thing any of us as bereaved parents need is a series of external expectations to meet to prove we are making progress. We are "bound" by grief; we didn't need to be "bound" by cultural norms as well.

Ernest Becker, in his Pulitzer Prize-winning book *The Denial of Death*, noted that the general public fundamentally denies death and resists the aura of recovery that surrounds anyone who has lost a loved one, particularly a child.[4] Many people think saying the child's name will make me cry, and they don't want that responsibility. Or they fear they will be drawn into a conversation about the death of children, which they would simply rather avoid. Becker noted that our consciousness is aware that anyone with children knows the fear of the death of a child, and perhaps the death of my child brings them relief that the death wasn't one of theirs. Having, or even thinking about this conversation, brings more anxiety to the non-bereaved.

Cultural norms change but have changed slowly. I sensed often a desire to return to normal as soon as possible. Once again wisdom came from the most unlikely of places. Two years ago, a widowed friend of mine was asked by her best friend if she was ready to date again. Her husband had been dead only a month. I'm not sure where from within these people these

4. Becker, *Denial* (eformat), location 158.

questions come. Perhaps each person surrounding the death wants things to return to normal as well. Friends want to return to playing cards, having dinner, and laughing. We try to bring intended relief. But instead, in closeness to the death of a child, we discover the experience to be shallow and seek the moment when we can graciously make our exit. The plans made, even when made by friends, emanate from a personal understanding of "normal" and generally come from a positive heart's desire. After all, they didn't lose a child and wish more than anything else that they could draw us back to the lightheartedness of life before all the events of those three years. But nothing takes the place of grief.

One couple with whom we had developed a new and fun friendship before Nicholas died became increasingly agitated with us as time moved on from his death. A year afterwards they shared that they realized that the experience of Nick's death was difficult, but they didn't understand why that kept us from reaching out and spending time with them. All explanations failed. Over time the friendship drifted further and further apart. That normal was gone, and whatever was going to replace that normal had yet to be born.

People struggle to withstand the constant experience of pain and suffering. Our work ethic leads us to believe there is nothing that cannot be overcome by hard work, discipline, and money. And yet, fundamentally I think America abhors suffering. As a result, we develop formulas for how to deal with life's difficulties. For example: A loved one dies and by the end of a year the bereaved "should" show signs of getting better, which includes no crying, no visits to the grave, perhaps new relationships, and no mention of the departed person's name. There is a sense that if we're not moving forward in culturally measurable ways, we're moving backwards; if you're not growing you're dying! What happens? Our grief goes underground—no pun intended.

As a baby boomer I think often of the Vietnam War and its aftermath. The only reason I didn't go was because President Nixon ended the draft while I was in college. Do you remember the struggle we had as a country welcoming home those who fought in that war? Something about hearing the death count for the day and the death count for the war on a daily basis desensitized us to the pain and suffering that all those deaths were causing throughout America, not to mention in Vietnam. When the war ended and the veterans returned home, there was no rejoicing or warm welcome. This only increased the despair experienced by so many regarding the war itself and bespoke a culture that didn't want to experience the trauma of death, particularly the deaths of so many young people.

In September of 2018 a friend of mine named Tom, who served in the Army and went to Vietnam, recounted an experience from the day he left Vietnam. DC-8 Stretches and 707 Stretches were used for the trips out of Vietnam and to Japan. The troops boarded the plane until every seat was taken. The flight to Japan from Saigon was around five hours. Suppressed silence filled the plane as the pilot taxied the craft to the runway, revving the engines to create the thrust that would bring these soldiers to freedom. The plane lumbered down the runway gaining speed, and the soldiers maintained nervous silence. As the plane climbed though the Vietnamese airspace each solider looked out the window engrossed in thoughts and reflections and yet feeling cautious about celebrating.

At about the halfway point of the flight, Tom remembered, "The pilot said the plane was functioning perfectly, however should a mechanical problem develop we'd passed the point of no return, and if a problem developed we would proceed to Yokato Air Force Base, Japan, rather than return to the republic of Vietnam. 'Welcome home!' The cabin erupted in an uproar of joy and release. The silence that enveloped the takeoff gave way to uncontrolled joy. There was no alcohol on the plane but we could smoke as much as we wanted. The plane was filled with blue smoke."

What struck me about Tom's story was that when he got to the part where it was announced that they never had to go back to Vietnam, he began to cry. Out of nowhere tears began to flow, which surprised him (and me). He couldn't believe he had made it; the stress and anxiety of war was over for him. He was really home. The memory of that moment invited the release of fear, sadness, and trauma that had continued to reside within a space of his spirit since that day.

Our culture would have said something was wrong with him. Grief set free honors the idea that experiences of trauma mark us for life and show up at the most interesting times. My friend Tom and I talked about this the next day. His tears reflected the joy he still feels daily for making it out alive —complete with the wife, children, and grandchildren that make his life so rich. He also thinks of all the soldiers who died and the many gruesome and violent memories of war. Those also have stayed with him all this time.

When someone asks me how many children I have, what's my answer? If I'm crying more than a year after my son's death, does that mean I've not "resolved" the grief? Do I stop saying my child's name? Do I worry about making other people uncomfortable? How do I live with a new definition of trivial matters of concern? Can I place myself in the shoes of someone who hasn't lost a child? What do I do with the tears, which have a mind of their own just like all the feelings of grief? Or the experience of being reminded of this loss and simply needing to be alone for a period of time? Not to mention the depression, emptiness, lack of energy, challenges of faith, raising other children, growing a marriage, and working?

With regularly having Tuesdays off, I would often take a child out for something special like bowling, visiting great-grandma, having lunch, following trucks, and more. A few weeks after Nick died, Hannah and I went to the bowling alley for a time together. The bumpers were set, and we bowled. I was grateful for Hannah and her companionship while, fast in the depths of grief, I willed myself to continue to step into life.

Even as I write this years later, I recall the feeling of despair within every sinew of my body. I recall the strength of will necessary to fight through the desire to remain in the house and delegate the care of Hannah to someone who had more life within. Some think that living on the edge of sorrow, with tears seeping from the eyes and sadness acting like suction drawing one's spirit into the shadows, carries no burden. Actions in that place are like going through the motions; they are actions of faith done in the hope that eventually there will be moments when the strain of grief and pain are forgotten, if even for a few seconds, and the spirit has a chance to breathe. We bowled.

Another woman who had been bowling in a woman's league picked up her toddler daughter on the way out. Her daughter was unhappy for some reason and didn't want to leave. The mother became increasingly frustrated with her and finally said, "Okay, Mommy's going to leave you, and no one will take care of you." I couldn't believe my ears. Years ago, her comments might have made sense, but in the context of the recent death of Nicholas I couldn't believe what she was saying. I thought that I'd gladly take her daughter home. I was also aware that she had no idea of the value and vulnerability of her child. She broke my heart. I got up and went over to the door and looked her in the eye with grief and anger. She had no idea of the gift she was holding by the hand, how swiftly life could take her assumption away and leave her with an empty hand searching for a connection that was gone forever.

More than anything else, this unknown woman reminded me that I had moved to a different place in the culture. I was and am well aware that I had no depth of understanding of the value of children and especially Nicholas, Hannah, and Zachary. I wondered if I'd look at children differently for the rest of my life. The answer is yes. But those who looked from the outside couldn't tell a thing unless they stood with me for a period of time. That choice was mine. I started to live my life with a secret that had the power to inspire, break, crush, identify, and more; that secret has the same power today. Today's culture reacts to news of the death of a child with speechless fear and anxiety. Our culture believes no worse loss exists than the loss of a child, and no pain is greater than the pain induced with the death of a child. At first, no doubt, this cultural norm mirrored experience. But now, thirty-one years later, grief invites no comparisons or competition.

Pain indicates something isn't right; some say pain is God's way of getting our attention about something in our lives that needs awareness. That is certainly true with my shoulder. My shoulder hurts and off to the doctor I go when the pain becomes unmanageable. An MRI reveals a slight tear in my rotator cuff tendon and lots of "junk" underneath the top. So when I move my arm a certain way the pain tells me now exactly what causes the pain and how to stop the pain. If I have surgery, "that" pain will go away. Our bodies are constantly communicating with us about places of vulnerability and wounding. Minds and hearts are the same.

While no one has seen a broken heart, every one of us knows what that feels like. There is a pain that indicates something isn't right and that pain reveals itself to us in the most vulnerable parts of our body and spirit. In the loss of a child, the "something" is the fact that the love of someone we love is no longer available to us in the flesh. That hurts. Pain is a constant companion after the death of a child. Most bereaved parents can tell you the day when they finally had a brief respite from the ache of loss.

One year at the National Conference of Compassionate Friends, I had an afternoon to myself and a chance to attend any workshop of my choosing. In a spirit of openness, I sought out the workshop that I thought would stretch my path of grieving. I attended a workshop on communication with the dead. Honestly, I wasn't nearly as open-minded as I professed but attended the workshop, nonetheless.

Two observations struck me right off the bat. First, the room was filled with bereaved parents seeking some way of being in touch with their departed child or children. Second, the people in the room were filled with measurable pain. The pain was heightened by fear of forgetting our departed children. Just recently I experienced an energy healing (Reiki) because of resistance to moving through grief once again. The masseuse kept telling me my son was waiting for me to connect with him and open up the pathways of connecting. And more recently Hannah had an experience in which she talked to Nicholas through an angel medium. She had a wonderful conversation in which they talked about Vickie's and my parenting, regarding Hannah. Nicholas told Hannah that we had done a great job parenting by letting her become her own person and not driving every day with fear.

Honestly. I don't know how to access this part of spirituality. While this isn't my experience, that doesn't make the experience false or crazy or unhelpful. Pain and tragedy often lead to desperation, which can lead us to explore options in grieving that we might not consider under other circumstances.

Grief is difficult enough without others judging our experiences. The rolling eyes of friends and family who think we are dragging this out in an unhealthy manner brings plenty of stress and emotional challenge. Navigating the new reality of one's life and the shift in principal relationships encourages all of us to find a path that leads to rest and relief. Caught in the grief from the death of my child is prison enough to live in. I don't need culture, in any form, to place constraints on my experience.

As long as anyone or any organization puts forth a formulaic path to recovery and healing those who agree with such a plan will find themselves in a prison of recovery. For me, the prison of recovery became the norm. I wanted out of prison! It was time to quit measuring growth by exploring the timelines of, or by seeking to live up to, cultural norms.

When I went to visit Bernard Ice, who is a medicine man, on a Lakota reservation in Minnesota, we talked, obviously, about my dead son and grieving. He asked me if I fed my son. I didn't know what he meant. "Do you leave him food so he can eat?" My resistance to the spiritual realm showed its ugly face again and while thinking this is crazy I said, "No, why?" Bernard asked, "What did he like to eat?" I answered that he loved Reese's Peanut Butter Cups. Bernard said, "Well, leave him some . . . feed his spirit and feed his spirit within you." I started leaving Reese's Cups for Nicholas every year either near his internment place or in the fields nearby.

Later than evening Bernard Ice held a sweat lodge for those of us from St. Michael's who wanted the spiritual experience. Initially this looked like a simple process; sit in the warm tent in the dark praying in Lakota and in English. While Bernard Ice was teaching me about seeing and feeding, the rest of the group was busy building a huge fire to warm the stones which would be used for the lodge.

Fr. Eagle Bull, the Episcopal priest on the reservation, invited me to have a talk before the lodge. He inquired if I had ever attended one before and the answer was no. He continued, "You cannot begin to imagine what you will experience in the lodge. You will discover paranoia, confusion, claustrophobia, fear, and pain like you've never experienced before in your life. You will sense many spirits and maybe even that of your son. You will be tempted several times to leave the lodge. You will recall experiences in your life long hidden. This will be unlike anything else you've done."

I was stunned. He couldn't be right. He hardly knew me. Or did he? I had no fears that he mentioned. Granted, I'm a bit obsessive-compulsive, but I thought that would help not hurt. The inability to see wouldn't trouble me nor would the reality of twenty people stuffed into a space meant to hold eight. I was ready, although I admit that even a closed MRI caused immeasurable anxiety. But a spiritual experience?

We entered the lodge, which looked like a small hut covered with layer after layer of animal skins. We sat knee to knee in two circles. We wore bathing suits. Once inside, those outside began to bring the rocks and place them in a hole in the middle. The rocks entered through the "door," a sacred pathway. There would be three doors. I didn't know what that meant. Fr. Eagle Bull suggested I sit right by the pit. My nerves tingled with excitement and yet a voice in the back of my head kept reminding me of my talk with Fr. Eagle Bull. I kept thinking he was off. I had that wrong.

Seated across the stones from Bernard Ice I watched, as we all did, the shuffling of the stones. While the door was open all seemed well. Heat surrounded us like a warm blanket on a cool fall evening. After all the rocks were placed, the door closed and the incredible journey began.

I had been in saunas and steam rooms, but the heat in this enclosure was unlike any of those experiences. And on top of that the sheer darkness made seeing anyone else impossible. Once we settled in, Bernard placed some tobacco on the stones and the embers became the only thing I could see. Soon he began chanting a prayer in his language. After a while we all attempted, at his invitation, to join him as we prayed for our ancestors and more.

At first the experience seemed interesting, but the challenges noted earlier by Fr. Eagle Bull didn't seem to be happening. Then as the heat began to soar and the sweat began to pour, anxiety attacked as a fight-or-flight scenario. My breathing intensified and with that the first signs of paranoia began to show. The walls seemed to close in, and the flight path looked appealing.

Attempts to control my breathing helped reduce the anxiety. As Bernard moved to praying for the dead tears began to flow in remembering Nicholas. The crying was uncontrollable and provided a means to "stay" within the first door of the lodge. Honestly, I didn't know there would be three sessions. I didn't know there would be three doors. The tears and the sweat mingled into a spiritual drink of centered paranoia; simply the fear of fear. And then came the first door.

The flap opened and fresh air circulated within the lodge. We drank deliciously cold water from a shared bowl using a shared ladle. The cool air brought a calming influence. Anxiety left when the door was opened. I had traversed the first door. The only challenge had been paranoia and anxiety. Fr. Eagle Bull asked me if I wanted to return for the second door. He discerned my fear and reluctance. I didn't want to return for fear of what demons awaited within my own spirit. After three minutes more rocks were added to the center hole, the door was closed, water poured over the rocks, and immediately heat surrounded and penetrated every pore.

It wasn't long before anxiety appeared again. Fear followed quickly on the wings of anxiety and as the temperature soared and the humidity increased, so did feelings of claustrophobia. We still sat knee to knee. Bernard began praying through chanting again. While listening my heart began racing, and I wondered how I'd ever endure the emotional onslaught until the door opened once again.

Soon, longing for Nicholas and the sheer sadness of his death collided with the claustrophobia, creating an internal conflict of immense proportions. Everyone in the lodge sensed this collision. While they prayed and often cried themselves, through Bernard their healing energy drew closer during prayer. They proved to be spiritual companions of all ages while my soul took a dive into hidden and unknown places of grief. One person's grief invited everyone's grief. We prayed, led by Bernard. All the while I remained in the grips of claustrophobia, vacillating internally between embracing spiritual intensity and the desire to get up and leave. Bernard knew. He slowly began to chant a prayer of peace and calm. Before I knew it, the flap was opened, and the second door ended. Tears subsided as the cool air washed over all of us in the lodge. Once again cool water passed from participant to participant. Bernard Ice shared that the third door lasted less time. Those words were no consolation. My heart and mind were exhausted, but with tired spirits and cramping legs we returned to our places.

Few memories come to mind of door three. The medicine man began gentle chanting. I sat there transfixed by the heat, the sound, the delicious smells, and the graceful chanting. Perhaps this door was a door of incorporation of all that had transpired before? And soon Bernard gave us water and shared with us the peace pipe containing very tasteful tobacco. The door was opened, and we exited exhausted but cleansed. Pain subsided for a while. Memories of Nicholas opened, flowing with grace and comfort. Sleep came easy that night. Quiet, deep, restful sleep.

Church members grieve in various ways. One woman whose husband died suddenly at a young age could not come back to the church after the funeral. In later conversation she stated, with tears, that returning to worship evoked an intolerable pain. A young woman who selectively reduced her fetuses from six to two in order that they and she might live, had the children baptized and then their family left the church. Another woman, upon entering the community room where her son's casket lay open, stepped in and began wailing inconsolably. The funeral attendants and church ushers immediately went to comfort her and to make sure she didn't fall. She asked me to walk with her and I did. She walked slowly and as tears turned to gentle sobs, we approached her son's casket. The wailing was accompanied by repeated touches of his body.

Churches, and perhaps other faith houses of worship, operate on a weekly cycle. Each Sunday people gather to worship, hear Scripture, pray, gossip, receive communion, satisfy curiosities about others, sing, drink coffee, and basically be community. But the key is that the cycle is weekly. Information from one week may or may not be considered in preparation for the following week. Those who die the previous week are mentioned in prayers, and names are written in the worship bulletin. The next Sunday the parish has moved on while the grieving family remains stuck in place, wondering why their loved one is no longer mentioned as their hearts are broken in two and still bleeding all over the pew.

Few churches are equipped with any sort of intentional ministry to the bereaved, believing that people will find their own way. There seems to be unawareness of the loneliness accompanying the journey. We go to church because we want community; we want to surround ourselves with people who might be willing to help us in our weakest moments. We wait and wait! Our own self-esteem or energy keeps us from asking, even though our hearts are breaking, for some little connection with another person around the loss of our child.

Religious institutions carry their own prescriptions of grief care and healing. For Christians the most popular comments focus on the child being in heaven, being in a better place, being completely healed, serving as a guardian angel, and more. While all this can be or is true, depending on your own belief, there is a disconnect between heavenly thoughts and the pragmatic reality that the child in the flesh is no longer alive or available. We all wish we could have just one more hug, one more day, and one more life.

Having such a religious cultural belief, which becomes a norm, permits those not directly affected by the loss to deal with their anxiety by placing the death in a place that allows them to move away from the experience. As I mentioned earlier, the most traumatic experience for a congregation is the death of a child.

Perhaps the norms exist in the church and in society due to the fact that the chaos of human grief, the depth of sorrow, and the despair of the human spirit are simply overwhelming for the majority of the public and must be contained somehow. The church serves to "contain" the experience by moving on. Or reminds us that life is dynamic, ever-changing.

Some priests long to be in the center aisle dressed in the finery and walking faithfully to exquisite music towards the sanctuary and the altar therein contained. Some of us live on the side aisle. While the center aisle looks beautiful, the situation presents no opportunity for freedom. One in the center aisle has abdicated self for a role in worship he or she is expected to serve with appropriate piety. Those of us on the side aisle occasionally yearn for the splendor of the center aisle; the key word is *occasionally*. Those on the side aisle are free to come and go as worship unfolds. We enjoy a bit of chaos and endure mistakes in pursuit of performance perfection. We can even look at the order of service and decide which parts to attend and/or participate in. The upside is freedom; the downside is the experience of being on the outside looking in on something special. Personally, I'm a side-aisle guy. Chaos invites opportunity as does tragedy. The metaphor works for bereaved parents in regard to cultural and religious norms.

Some experiences in life present us with situations that prove difficult to "fix" in any neat and orderly way, and whose effects linger for years or even decades. They simply won't fit into any preconceived box, even the beauty and grace of the church, even the center aisle. In a culture driven to move forward at all costs, the poor bereaved parent trying to put their life together must resist the temptation to accede to cultural norms and follow the freedom of their heart while loving their departed child or children. Follow the freedom of their heart. Follow the freedom of my heart. Become a side-aisle person.

It's too easy to say all expectations from others serve as projections of the bereaved or the circle of the bereaved. It has been my experience that there is no one single formula that invites each bereaved parent to find a way to heal. We each grieve in our own way. Cultural and religious norms tend to force expressions of long-term healing into hiding. This is partly because life is continuously ongoing and unfolding and partly because although most of us are fine with the acute moments of grief right after the loss, we tend to be uncomfortable with the chronic life of grief that extends indefinitely into the future.

The Big Book of Alcoholics Anonymous states that when it comes to growth in the spiritual life, the goal is "progress not perfection."[5] This truth extends to long-term grief as well. When the alcoholic enters into sobriety he or she wishes to remain in sobriety for the rest of their lives. They wake up each day an alcoholic but believe that with the support of a higher power and a circle of like-minded folks they can go another day without drinking. The program also calls for openness to continual growth.

It's because so many of us are driven by perfection that the *Big Book* proclaims the desire to be "progress not perfection." And such is true with grief. We bereaved parents wake up each day as a bereaved parent. We are many other things, but we are bereaved parents; I wake up every day a bereaved parent reaching out to my son Nicholas, giving him into God's hands, and hoping to grow just a bit in grief and renewal. We as bereaved parents desire progress not perfection as the norm. No one wishes to remain stuck but that "something" happens. Recovering alcoholics call these periods "dry drunks." They often happen because we don't pay attention to what has helped us get to where we are in our lives, and we slip into old patterns of behavior without drinking. Let's try that center aisle one more time.

Certainly, the same can occur with bereaved parents, and over time we can also find resources and friends and maybe even a God who can draw us towards a new level of acceptance and joy over our child. This may sound like a miracle to you and it is. But as long as we listen most carefully to this different and often hidden cultural norm of "progress not

5. Alcoholics Anonymous, *Big Book*, 66.

perfection," our hope of growing into the story of our lives, which includes the death of our child, increases.

Chapter 11

Shattered Fragments of the Soul

This, then, is what I understand by making space for a heart—
close-to-cracking: the space where we learn to forge a way of talking about God in the midst of the ruins of the forms of the sacred
which are in full collapse.[1]

WHEN GRANDPA WEISE DIED I was ten years old. Repeatedly at the wake
and funeral people kept wondering why I was so sad. They believed I didn't
know him nearly as well as they did. Except I did. He was disabled, having lost a leg to diabetes. Mom would often take me to his home and he
would take care of me. He was a devoted Chicago Cubs fan and we watched
baseball together. Yes, watched? The black-and-white TV had to be two feet
long and eighteen inches wide to hold all the parts necessary to produce a
screen about eighteen by eighteen inches. There were four stations, including WGN, channel 9, home of the Cubs. I have no idea how many hours we
spent together.

When the time came to close the casket I shook away from my family
and ran up to grab my grandpa and hold on for life. Adults wondered about
such a display of grief. My parents came and helped me let go, tending to
me in the inconsolability of my tears. Today his memory continues as a gift,
and my hope is that Nicholas has met my grandpa in the beyond. As a child,
I didn't understand anything but love and loss.

Several years later, my Grandma Johnson died. She was a deeply faithful woman. After marrying my grandfather, she did, as women did in 1918,
take on the faith of her husband. That faith was Swedish Covenant. She

1. Alison, *Faith*, 34.

84

was immediately excommunicated from the church of her upbringing, the Wisconsin Synod Lutheran Church. That had no effect on her faith. She remained a faithful believer all her life. When her husband died in 1981 her life goal was to be with "Dad" again. One day in March of 1986, after stopping her heart medicine, unknown to any of us, she put on her best dress, went into their bedroom, laid down on the bed, and died. The broken heart finally cracked, and she became ready to leave.

Broken-openedness, as James Alison writes, doesn't consist of one incident, but several incidents of pain over a period of time, each putting a crack in our souls. For Alison the pain came from the repeated unwillingness of the Catholic Church to accept that he was both a priest and gay. The official position was that no gay people were allowed to serve as priests. Alison was a side-aisle person. He challenged the duplicity of decrying homosexuality while a significant percentage of clergy were gay. He wanted to be a priest with his entire person. Every time they sought to take the gift of priesthood away from him, he fought back, continuing as a priest. And yet each time he was rejected his heart broke again, until the experience became the broken-openedness of his life.

Several years after Nicholas died the entire vestry (board) and staff of St. Michael's went on retreat. Our leader was a deacon in the Roman Catholic Church. His spirituality was simple and deeply faithful. One session he focused on forgiveness. Each person as the meditation unfolded and the silence ensued was welcome to come forward to a large flat pan that was filled with smooth sand. He said, "Come on forward and write the names of anyone you believe you need to forgive. Write them one at a time and then smooth the name out and add any others." Immediately my hackles went up and interior defenses created instantaneous walls of protection. In no way was I going to participate in any such frivolous and futile exercise.

After a period of uncomfortable silence, one of the vestry members went up to the sand and stood there with her hands by her sides. Slowly she put her hand in the sand and began writing names and erasing them, writing and erasing, writing and erasing. Within a few minutes she was crying but the tears seemed to be tears of relief. Then another member went forward and immediately wrote and erased once. He returned to his seat showing no emotion. Then another and another, and most seemed to have an incredible encounter with God and themselves.

Defenses wore down, I approached the sand. My list began with the usual suspects: Mom, Dad, Brent, Julie, Carl, Leslie. Then things turned and as my hand went to write the name of God in the sand, tears began to flow unchecked. The response surprised me. The tears kept coming and coming such that I could hardly see the sand. I erased God and put Nicholas's name. What could I possibly need to forgive Nicholas for? Dying. Now with more tears and smoothing the sand, the last name I put in the sand was me; I needed to forgive myself for many things in life and especially for all I did that wasn't helpful with Nicholas.

Like others, I returned to my seat appreciating the silence. In truth, the silence felt as if God surrounded me in grace. After all those who wished to go to the sand were finished, the deacon sat with a bit more silence and then concluded with a brief prayer. We rose from our chairs with lesser burdens than when we started. Lunch followed and we walked to lunch as a group with the laughter and community that often follows times of collective vulnerability. The remainder of the retreat has vanished from memory. But the sand has remained all these years later. Forgiving myself took more time, but the seeds of healing took hold.

James Alison wrote of the broken-openedness of the human soul, how the life we were living breaks into fragments and then we wait to see what might be created from the pieces. There is a story about an English cathedral several centuries ago and a young apprentice working with stained glass. He wanted so much to do his own work, but the nature and scope of the undertaking simply relegated him to be an apprentice. Finally, he persistently asked if he could make a little something for the cathedral from the fragments of glass that had been discarded. The leader consented and so the boy went to work. After a time, he was all excited and asked if he could show his work. With that exasperation of experience, the leader said yes, and the boy presented an exquisitely beautiful circular window that was actually placed in the cathedral.

The reality that my heart had been broken into pieces by Nicholas's death took a long time to settle in. This was a disguised attempt to reopen the old door and return to the way it was, a hope that the old ways would work. I sat in this orange chair I have and asked God to help me because I was unable to live this path on my own. God held me while I watched my soul shatter right before my eyes.

One time, a retreat leader took the sheets of paper that represented our dreams and dropped them on the floor. I picked them up. He said that was significant. I wondered. As I sat in the orange chair, the pieces of my soul, my very self, were scattered around the floor. There was no energy and no way to pick them all up. I sat there wondering, how would God choose to begin putting Humpty Dumpty back together again? If only this could be reduced to a well-planned intellectual exercise.

As life moved on from that original life-shattering event, parts of me did not move on so quickly. I presented a recognizable picture on the outside but inside I continued to scramble to hold the pieces together, seeking to avoid continued breakdowns. And yet they happened. For me, they took place often in the car listening to music. Out of nowhere thoughts and feelings of Nicholas would overwhelm me and the tears would begin to flow. My wife Vickie cried regularly in the shower. Some people would go sit in their dead child's room and there take a deep breath and allow their brokenness to unfold and rest. We often chased away our tears in hopes of getting ahead of the pain and brokenness, only to discover that a broken heart mends on its own time.

Several years after Nicholas died and after the end of a particularly intense work experience, I arrived home to an empty house. It had been nine years since Nick had died and all seemed well. Then, I looked at a certain picture and the tears began to flow, accompanied by pains of grief that made me choke and nearly throw up, the coughing and the sobs were so deep and primitive. No matter how much I tried, I could not get the crying to stop. Just when it seemed that my heart and soul calmed down, the next wave of grief would come and overwhelm me once again with tears too deep for words. Four hours later I finally calmed down enough to prepare to meet my parents for dinner at their local country club, which required about a thirty-mile drive.

Once I calmed down and was in the car, all went well except that I had left so early that I needed to kill some time. So I stopped at a bookstore on the way. Five minutes inside the store, the sobs returned, and it was all I could do to run back out, climb into my car, put my head down, and surrender to the sadness once again. About thirty minutes later the crying slowed to the point where I could drive again.

I made it to my parents' country club where, upon parking the car, I broke into uncontrollable sobs for the third time that day—uncontrollable! Finally, the tears subsided long enough for me to leave the car and head inside. My mom asked me how my day was, and I shared with her about my difficulties. She then noted that if I thought that was something, I should have seen what her day was like. Her apparent insensitivity settled me down. Later that night I could see the pieces of my soul scattered before me on the floor, and the fact that they were all over the place didn't frighten me anymore. In time, and with the help of God and others, the pieces would find their way back together; but the stained glass circle they would create would be far different from the previous picture.

We have a beautiful St. Nicholas statue given to us by the church I was serving when Nick died. It has been broken three times in the past twenty-five years. It never shattered, however. Little breaks can generally be repaired but the original cracks will still show up, regardless of how well the repairs are made. The reason the cracks still show up is that we know where to look for them. And if you've ever broken a piece of pottery you know the impossibility of drawing the pieces back into a coherent whole. It's more likely you will simply let that go and perhaps replace the mug with another one that is similar, or maybe not similar at all. No matter what path is taken, deep inside we know that the past has been broken into infinite pieces like the shattering of the mug; and the truth is that while the infinite pieces cannot be forged back together, there is a memory of who we are and where we have been that enables us to pick out a new mug that connects to a shared past in ways that our internal life recognizes and accepts.

Chapter 12

About God

Your conscious and loving existence gives glory to God.[1]

BEACHES IN THE NEW England area are different creatures than in the Caribbean. The sky is often gray, the waves pound away, sometimes violently and relentlessly, and the sand of the beach has a different color than the Caribbean, like wheat or soybeans. People often go to the beach regardless of the weather. As it happened the retreat center I was attending in New England provided rides to the beach for quiet and walking. Brother Martin dropped me off and said he'd be back in an hour . . .

In the book *Meditations for Bereaved Parents*,[2] one of the contributors shared this story. Seeking to recover from the death of his daughter and longing for any sign, he went swimming in the Gulf of Mexico off the coast of Florida. He prayed, "Lord, if my daughter is OK and you're going to help me heal, let me reach into the water and find a sand dollar." He reached into the water and behold he found one. Being an evangelical Christian, he was a deep believer. But then this: "Thank you God, but if you're really there I will reach my other hand down into the water and find another sand dollar." He did and found another. Quietly he thanked God and returned to his seat on the beach. His heart took great comfort from this experience.

Back to the beach in New England. Overcast skies and a violent ocean greeted the beach that day. Occasionally rain fell, but nothing to stop further walking and silence. Remembering the above story, I began looking

1. Rohr, *Falling*, xxix.
2. Osgood, ed., *Meditations*, 47.

for sand dollars, searching for the same sense of God's presence that he had looked for. After twenty minutes or so, tucked by a pool of water, I spotted a sand dollar. The dollar was large and dark compared to those I found on other beaches. (I didn't know that they all come this color and are bleached white by the sun.)

As the evangelical above, one wasn't enough for me. I said, "If you're really here, God, and attending to my broken heart, I need to find the second sand dollar." I scoured the beach in search of proof of the existence of God. Eyes down searching and searching, I knew there would not be a second shell. Then, right there in front of me rested a second dollar. At first I looked around to see if there were more. The proof, you see, was only in finding one. There were no others nearby, so I picked up the second one (I still have both of them). My heart wanted so much to believe throughout the years following Nicholas's death, and that proved to be a struggle. My tears drew me to God and yet, and yet!

Through sobs, I began furiously scouring the beach for one more sand dollar so my anger and frustration with God could be justified. Maybe I was blind by sadness or tears or hope, but regardless I never found a third sand dollar. Tears of anger turned to tears of gratitude and contentment. How does anyone discern the presence of God? Do you and I hear directly? Do we see a sign? Do we hear through someone else? I don't know. That day the serendipity, God's way of remaining anonymous, took me by the hand and presented God right before my face as I stood alone in the sand with two sand dollars, on an overcast day in Massachusetts with tremendous waves crashing on the shore.

Later, after I became sober in January of 1999, the time came for me to take the third step in my recovery. This step says, "Made a decision to turn our will and our lives over to the care of God *as we understood him.*"[3] I couldn't face this step. I kept playing hide-and-seek with my sponsor, Joe C. One day I looked up from my desk at St. Michael's and Joe marched himself right into my office. "It's time to do your third step!" he said. I replied, "You know, Joe, I got issues. I got issues with God. I mean one of my kids died and all. I don't know." He took my hand and we knelt right there and prayed the third step prayer, "God, I offer myself to Thee to build with me and to do with me as Thou wilt. Relieve me of the bondage of self, that I may better do Thy will. Take away my difficulties, that victory over them may bear witness to those I would help of Thy power, Thy love, and Thy Way of life. May

3. Alcoholics Anonymous, *Big Book*, 59 (emphasis original).

I do Thy will always."[4] And just like that Joe was gone. Developing a belief about God after Nicholas's death didn't have to be complicated but did need to be honest and forthright.

Joel Primack suggested in *The View from the Center of the Universe* that each of us take a moment to lie on the ground, look up to the sky, and appreciate the fact that the world is rotating and yet we don't feel the rotation. He also said to imagine being deep in space observing the world. From that distance there are no borders or boundaries, no ability to discern the color or age or religious beliefs of people. Seas and land look as they must have in the beginning of creation, discernible only by differing colors. Primack presents the reality that we are all part of something greater than ourselves, however you wish to describe that "greater." He contends that earth isn't the final expression of the cosmos, but simply another participant in the ever-evolving universe which we share with all other beings and things that are stardust.[5] The universe is expanding, he states, and the expansion includes us.

For a moment on that beach I became aware of being a part of something much greater than myself. But while I only had a little part, I still had a part. The movement of creation comforted my spirit, and I realized we come and go and give what we can to life and try to let life go as best we can. The point is this: there's my economy and God's economy. They aren't the same. In my economy Nicholas didn't receive all that he "should have" received, even though for the years he lived, his life was rich with love and joy. In God's economy perhaps life isn't viewed in the same way. Watching a small wildebeest separated from the herd and eaten by a group of wild dogs reminds me that all life participates in life; both those who live and those who die, which, of course, means all of us.

All this is to say that quite possibly in God's economy Nicholas lived a full life. The struggle with being an American and exploring grief focuses on my tendency to want to value something by quantity; more life is better and less life is worse. Perhaps our fear of death, perhaps my fear of death, invites the urge to desire more; to define the quality of life by how many years I get to live. In so doing, what am I missing? I think I'd be missing the love and the beauty of any day. My friend Terry Parker, God rest his soul, as he was dying noted that the most difficult part of dying was saying goodbye to loved ones. That's the "never" on the other side of the equation. Terry

4. Alcoholics Anonymous, *Big Book*, 63.

5. Primack and Abrams, *View from the Center*, 89.

knew he wouldn't get to see many things in his family's life. As he died he asked me to take care of his family. I have failed.

Do we leave this life thinking "I've been screwed" or "This is so inadequate"? Or plagued by regrets, resentments, and anger? Elisabeth Kubler-Ross noted that the last phase of recovery in grief is acceptance. This is the great hurdle bereaved parents struggle to embrace. The discipline to seek such heroics only exhausts the human spirit and continuously says that the cup is forever half empty.

Two sets of parents (couple one and couple two) experience the brutal death of their two children who were in love and killed in an accident. Several different paths towards healing take place. The first and most obvious is the set of parents who invest themselves in the court process. The process demands that they keep themselves angry. When a member of the other family begins to soften a bit, the anger of couple one leads them to cut off the relationship with couple two. When couple two explores forgiveness, the wife cannot, and the husband isn't sure. Eventually, as the man in couple two explores forgiveness, his wife leaves him. Later the man finds not only forgiveness, but more importantly, peace. Parents who lose a child to a drunk driver often focus their anger and potential for healing in the judicial process. Or, after that, they take up the cause of, for instance Mothers Against Drunk Driving. That's definitely a worthy cause, but the last time I presented at their national workshop the leader was still so angry about the death of her son. She failed to consider that perhaps those in attendance were there because they knew she would unconsciously enforce their desire to keep their child's memory alive by anger. Yet several parents clearly showed disagreement by their attendance or, shall I say, their absence. They simply stopped coming to the workshops and focused instead on gaining support for their grief over drinks or dinner. Anger blinds us. Anger blinded me. The seduction of anger is that perhaps by anger we can see the cup as half full. I don't think so. The cup may appear half full, but the drink is anger and once the anger dissipates what's left is not just a half empty cup, but an empty cup. And all the waves of grief locked behind the wall of anger explode, like a tsunami, and we bereaved parents drown in our grief.

The importance of acceptance is the role acceptance plays in the movement towards joy, forgiveness, and gratitude. These gifts to the bereaved evaporate with sustained anger. They become dormant, awaiting light, water, tilling, and more.

In ego psychology there are three levels of meaning to any aspect of life. The first level is the manifest level; this is the level we can see, hear, taste, touch. The second level is the symbolic level; this is the level where the experience begins to take on meaning unique to the individual. The third, and deepest level, is the analeptic level; this is the level where the experience connects with our deepest selves to form identity.

For me, each level of meaning regarding God was firmly fixed before Nicholas got sick and died. Like many new pastors I thought it was more important to talk to my parishioners about the need to pray but rarely prayed myself. But here's what unfolded.

In 1972, on an oil rig in the Gulf of Mexico, an explosion took place on the platform where I worked. Fortunately, the team averted disaster by getting the leak under control, but not before closing every well on the platform and not before trying to piece together tattered nerves. That night when I went to sleep I said my childish prayers for the first time in years, believing that I'd be protected if I said my prayers: "Now I lay me down to sleep . . ." Simple. I did not explore beyond the manifest level.

In 1973 as my life was heading down the drain, God became the direction of my life. The manifest moved to the symbolic. In need of forgiveness, love, and community, I started attending a local church in Tulsa and began opening myself to God and God to myself. In so doing the earlier manifestation of God ceased.

When I entered seminary, I fought such deep concerns as my worthiness and sinfulness; I learned how much I didn't know about philosophy and theology; I learned that believing in God wasn't necessarily important; and the only path of redemption in front of me was ordination—the symbolic became analeptic and God took a place in my heart and I took a place in God's heart.

When Nicholas died all three levels were shattered and there was nothing with which to replace them. The broken-openedness James Alison mentions in *Faith Beyond Resentment* became a living truth. The challenge focused on trying to project a life of faith to those I served while unable to piece together the fragments of my own soul. When Nicholas's breath ceased a void took shape in my soul, vying to be filled in some way. And yet the old God would not "fit" anymore. I continued preaching and teaching and leading worship, trusting that God could and would use me in spite of my personal agnosticism, anger, and despair. Square peg. Round hole.

I love being a parish priest. That vocation seems to be what I was born to become and something for which I am grateful. Priesthood has taken me into the lives of people in ways that I never imagined, allowing me to see both the joy as well as the sorrow of human existence. I've sat with many people who have wondered about the face of God in the midst of tragedy and trauma, personally and in the larger world. For years I thought an answer to this complicated question was expected of me and so I offered answers. I used then what I consider throwaway (manifest) lines like "God never gives us more than we can handle." (Really? God looks at each of us, assesses us, determines what we can handle, and then goes to work testing the proposition?) I said it was God's will. (Do I want a God who wills suffering and pain on people?) I said, "You're young and you can have more children." (This one embarrasses me the most, having used that seemingly comforting line with a couple who had just experienced a miscarriage.) There was more noise, simple religious slogans attempted to thwart the painful and necessary process of human grief. If you're a Christian and believe your child is in heaven, that's fine, but we still grieve the child's absence in the flesh. Many will say he's in a better place, but no one wishes their child to get there any time soon. Knowledge of heaven may console the mind and heart, but grief will continue to mark the soul. Such is life. There are no exceptions.

Death, especially the death of a child, shattered my theology about God. Grief demands a new doctrine of God that incorporates more of life than before and leaves places for growth, healing, and discovery. This isn't easy if one holds anger and resentments towards God. Here I speak from experience. If I'm honest the question of God and Nicholas's death still evokes wonderment at creation and God's role in our lives, and resentment, at times, that life is what life is. Albert Einstein believed that there was a divine presence behind the creation of the universe and the laws which governed it. But surely he believed that said God could intervene in that order and change the order whenever he, as the Divine, wished. Michael, a friend and priest, believes God can intervene at any time and heal a broken spirit. And there are others. I wonder.

In Genesis we hear a story of Jacob wrestling with God. I wonder what Jacob was wrestling with God about when he was wounded. I bet Jacob initiated the wrestling match over something having to do with some mystery of life or something about life he simply thought should be different. At any rate, he invites God to wrestle over the outcome. He learned something in that exchange that remained with him for the rest of his life, in spite of all his wives and children. He also ended with a limp. Unbeknownst to Jacob, his vulnerability was readily available to God and so God touched him there, and he was painfully reminded daily that he was human.

Job lost everything he valued. I wonder what Job felt when he got to the end of all his friend's arguments about why he suffered so much in his life. I think Job got angry and courageously took his anger directly to God. And God responded. God told Job to gird his loins and sit down, as he was about to be reminded about who Job was and what was his to know and what wasn't for him to know. That was the extent of what God would reveal. What appears as a humiliation is actually liberation. Job doesn't have to know any answer; he simply needs to believe in himself and the God who helped bring him into being, and he needs to step forward.

On March 26, 1989, Vickie and I sat on the front sidewalk of our home in Bloomingdale. Young Hannah was running with her friends, laughing and having a ball. Vickie and I sat on the cool sidewalk watching the sun disappear into the western horizon. The weather had been unusually warm that Easter and it seemed the entire neighborhood poured forth into the streets to catch a glimpse of the warmth to come. Gazing upon the sunset, I said, "What do you think Nicholas sees?" Vickie replied, "I think he sees a sunset more beautiful than anything we could ever imagine in this life." I added, "What if dead is dead is dead?" She answered, "That may be true, Al, but I choose to believe in the resurrection; I choose to believe he is with God."

Just about everyone has a theology about God and just about all think their theology is true not only for themselves, but for everyone. While I was leading a spirituality panel with three other theologians the following took place. We opened the floor to questions. This person in his late fifities stood up and said, "After 9/11 my son decided to become a marine. He went through all his training and deployed to Iraq. People from all over the world were praying for him. Now he's dead." And he sat back down.

The entire room was paralyzed. Like many other visions of God, he couldn't place this outcome in his belief, and he wanted our help. The four of us all faced the audience and could not make eye contact with each other. Silence seemed to last forever. Finally, a member of the panel began by saying how sorry she was for his loss and asked his son's name. It was Peter. Silence returned. I said, "I don't know what to say. I suspect you think I can answer this question because I'm a priest, but I've also lost a child and any of the cliché answers seem inadequate." He gently waved me off. Others tried to console him with phrases like "God is with you in your suffering." "God was always with him." "Free will brings good and bad." All inadequate. We were relieved when another person grabbed a microphone and changed the subject.

In another small group setting a woman shared the following: "My son George was killed in a horrible accident in Georgia about six months ago. Needless to say, my family and I were devastated. Within a week of George's death, a dear friend of mine, a friend from the Baptist church we attended, asked me if George was baptized and did he ask Jesus to be his personal savior. Well, I knew George wasn't an active churchgoer or believer for all I knew, and I told her so. She responded by saying, 'We all know where he is. He's in hell.' I looked around the room and sought the closest exit, ran outside, and dissolved into heaving sobs. I wondered if that could be true? Was that the God I'd been following my entire life? A God who would reject my beautiful son because he struggled with believing? I never went back to that church and nobody ever called me. My faith in God is stronger now than my faith has ever been."

Christians are notorious for seeking to give comfort by these words, "Well, at least they are in a better place." There's an old joke about a preacher leading a revival about salvation. He gets the crowd all fired up and says, "Stand up right now if you want to go to heaven." Everyone stands up but this older man in the front row. The preacher says, "Don't you want to go to heaven?" "Oh yes, yes," the old man replies, "I just don't want to be first in line."

In another case there was a lady named Debra and she was Jewish. People kept saying to her, "Well, at least your son is in a better place." (He was a three-year-old boy who climbed on a chest and the chest fell and crushed him.) Not one to mince her words, she said, "If my child is in such a better place, why don't you go home, kill your children, so they can also be in a better place?" What a great conversation ender. Yet she made sense and made it clear to those using such platitudes that they didn't make sense and were not comforting.

And finally, our dear attending physician, Dr. Susan Cohn, was heart stricken when the time came for us to take Nicholas home to die. I asked her, knowing she was Jewish, "Do you believe in heaven?" She answered, "No, but if I were experiencing what you're experiencing I'd probably begin to explore eternity." She was an angel. How much of our or my belief in God comes from contemplative time or intellectual time or human experience or desperation? Discovering a new and sustaining belief in God became a wonderful journey of discovery.

Chapter 13

Silence

Now there was a great wind . . . but the Lord was not in the wind; and after the wind an earthquake, but the Lord was not in the earthquake, and after the earthquake a fire, but the Lord was not in the fire; and after the fire a sound of sheer silence. When Elijah heard it, he wrapped his face in his mantle and went out and stood at the entrance to the cave.[1]

IMAGINE SITTING IN THE front row in a wonderful theatre. Several people have asked for a chance to pitch their case for God. They know our previous beliefs no longer suffice and they, from the depths of their hearts, seek to share their insights with us. Vickie and I struggled to replace a relationship with God not only for healing, but also to direct our lives for years to come. One by one the various advocates carefully chose their times to let us in on their understanding in hopes that might help pull us out of our pain and a sense of the absence of God.

Paula introduced us to the God of practical justice: "an eye for an eye, and a tooth for a tooth, and a life for a life." She especially wondered if Nick's death reflected God's justice: take a life; lose a life; a kind of punishment for previous sins; God's balance of justice. She wondered, without saying, if there was some sin back there in our lives for which this would serve as justice. Hers appeared as a seemingly easy interpretation that this was God's justice, that we were being punished for earlier sins. Once she finished she stood there staring at us with a righteous look on her face. I could not hide the incredulity. The problem was that I did have some good

1. 1 Kings 19:11–13.

sins in my life and had to fight the impulse to believe what she was suggesting. Luckily more advocates for God showed up also. Paula left the stage and took a seat in the first balcony.

Tim presented the God of puppetry. This was interesting. The God of puppetry. Tim is an actor, so his presentation thought this God rules over creation with the strings of a puppeteer managing the moves of every person and bringing about losses and gains as part of a plan to teach us, or someone, some lessons. He laughingly said, "Well, you know, sometimes the strings get tangled." While this belief showed a God appearing somewhat punishing, all suffering was presented as essential for the purification of sinners. We could relax in the knowledge that all was held in the hands of God who brought about such action as God's will for the projected betterment of all. Tim joined Paula in the balcony.

And then there was Ben. He shyly presented the God of enough prayer. He confused me at first because I couldn't understand what he was asking me and/or telling me. He asked if Vickie and I prayed? Yes. He asked if we had been praying enough; had Vickie been praying enough? Oh so subtly, the real purpose of the question became clear. This was actually more of an assessment and judgment, and we were found guilty. He believed, and said, that I hadn't prayed enough. He believed that if I had prayed enough, together with the thousands of people around the world praying for Nicholas, certainly that was enough to keep him alive, wasn't it? I asked him, "Ben, do you think I didn't pray enough? That Nicholas died because I didn't pray enough?" He nodded his head. Had I prayed enough to spare Nicholas's life? Truthfully I didn't know. Ben and the God who measured life's consequences through prayer joined Paula and Tim.

The next presentation actually came from a group of people. Five people walked on to the stage led by a man who once taught about religion and spirituality at our local high school. They were also shy at first. Perhaps they wondered how I'd respond. As it turned out, they were all agnostic. The agnostics wanted to make sure their view of the God of indifference also showed up and got a fair hearing. Basically, this God served as a benign presence over creation with little affect or interest in the details. This God remained hidden beyond responsibility and judgment. This God got lost in the black hole of the cosmos. No tears were shed by this God for losses. God's indifference only exceeded our incapacity to know God.

This group piqued my curiosity. I had spent countless hours viewing and reviewing the "why" question of Nicholas dying and believed that any new belief in God had to address this question in a way that freed me from expectations. No more burdening myself with additional layers of guilt and personal responsibility. The agnostics received a bit more time on stage than the others. They were asked to take a seat on the back of the main floor.

Now Anger appeared on my internal stage with no invitation or clear entrance. I could not tell if that was anger at God or if God was somehow simply angry. I was blind on this one. Anger hardened me into an obelisk, paralyzing motion and forcing repeated alterations of my internal perception. Anger built upon anger resulted in a wave of self-justification requiring stability and not movement; my ego became delusional. In this space something had to become the focus of the anger. The feeling was, in many ways, primitive. I didn't turn back, but I remained stuck in a revolving reality that continuously looked different through the eyes of the anger. Is there a God of anger? This one simply stayed nearby.

We travel the path of grief alone and yet hopefully in the company of loved ones and some spiritual reality. No one can process my feelings but me and I wonder if sharing them with others heals. I think so. Suffering mitigated anger. To ask the "why question" encompasses asking about the existence of suffering and our inevitable experience of it. The source of most anger in grief is suffering and I would rather be angry. There is power in anger. There is humility in suffering. There is death in anger. There is life in suffering. There is frustration in anger. There is joy in suffering. None of this is supposed to make sense either. I wondered if I could just shut up. And then Maria appeared onstage.

Maria asked if she could have some time on stage. We agreed because we had known her for years, but not her beliefs about God. Much to our surprise, she said there is no God. She wasn't angry and she wasn't trying to convert us into not believing in God if we so chose. She offered that the experiences of this world were only of this world and therefore even more acute to our experience of them. She found comfort and strength in gratitude for a life well lived and in the circle of love that held her close in moments of excruciating pain. She was a scientist. She was an astronomer. She said that Nick, like all people and all things, was made of stardust among many other things: atoms, molecules, fractals, and more. All things are made of stardust. Nicholas has joined a larger reality. I asked, "Isn't that God?" And Maria answered, "No, that is simply life." I gave her a seat near the stage and asked her to stay for awhile.

My struggle deepened. By now Vickie had experienced this dream. Vickie was seated in one of our blue recliners in the family room of the rectory in Barrington. As she sat there Nicholas appeared with Jesus. Slowly, Nick let go of Jesus' hand and walked over to his mom and said, "Don't worry, Mommy, I'm fine and I'm right here in this new house with you." He smiled and awaited the confirmation of her smile. Then he turned and looked at Jesus, who beckoned him to come along and they walked away holding hands. That vision, combined with her simple yet profound belief that Nicholas lived in the heart of God, brought her a deep serenity. That was enough for her. With her acceptance came a peace. I was jealous. Yet, she sat with me as the interviews continued.

The stage remained empty. The presented Gods so far represented false gods, each vying to import a simple explanation on a complex and painful human experience of suffering and loss. I had only an occasional temptation to believe these false gods because each one touched upon a place of my culture and upbringing; my own expectations as well as those of my parents and grandparents; a simple hope that maybe God was in charge, so I didn't have to be, or perhaps there was a simple answer for life's complicated experiences. I wondered. I hadn't really needed God in any way besides forgiveness or fear management up to this point in my life, so my theology proved inadequate time and time again. I knew that but never explored anything different. After all, I was seminary taught and trained; I had studied systematic theology where all truth aligned; I understood.

Grief healing can be like that; minutes feel like hours. The world passed us by and if anyone was challenged by our struggle with belief about God, no one said anything to us. Mostly expectations grew that we would move on and put this behind us. Theology, God, isn't that easy. The deep questions persisted. Other gods, more inquisitive and friendly gods, began to show up on this makeshift stage.

The next group to present were personally invited. At the base level I believe God does not inflict sorrow and suffering on anyone. If there are such things as free will and chaos theory and the laws of the universe, life goes where life wills and there will always be aberrations, one-offs, perversions, imperfections, and chance. Next up, Jeff Goldblum.

My favorite character in the original *Jurassic Park* is the Jeff Goldblum character, who consistently places before the developers the reality of chaos theory. All of a sudden there he was onstage asking if I wanted to visit. He argued, what is love if love isn't given freely to the beloved? If my love is

conscripted, then love is cheap. The choosing to love someone and the sur-
rendering to that power greater than ourselves that opens up our hearts and
lives to the world and all that the world, even the universe, is about, can also
come crashing down just like the fences in the movie. Goldbum's character
challenged me to enter into an open relationship with God, seeking to accept that life is chaotic, and that Divine Love, given and accepted, seeks to
help guide our path. He got a seat in the family section.

Then Jim showed up. He said that God is present with me in moments of suffering and sorrow working with my heart and soul to discover
a continued renewal of life and hope. God isn't love but God sends love and
God could be life and could desire life, and a full life, for all God's creation,
including me. There are hurdles. The world is a place of predators and prey,
where we constantly must consume in order to live. And we also must die
in order to live. The cycle proved difficult to accept when the cycle involved
those closest to me.

This belief in God was easier to live with than the others; at least this
God suggested I was part of the creative mix of life and had responsibility
for my choices and myself. I long ago understood that if life, love, and creation were free, they had to be free in all circumstances. And while perhaps
an omnipotent God could enter into creation on a whim, that didn't appear
to be the way God loved God's creation.

Laurie looked around the curtain and asked if we would see her. She
taught that as the need to seemingly be in control of grief subsided, ever so
slowly the God of companionship and compassion began to be revealed,
more compassion than companionship. I had sought to go this path alone
but could not. As noted earlier, Fr. Roy joined my life and brought consolation and companionship as I struggled through the excruciating pain of
human grief and the silence of God. I asked Roy for his answers. All Roy
did was lay hands upon my head and ask for God's healing and encouraged
me to take a nap, have a lemon drop, relax my expectations, and love.

Soon enough Michael appeared and with him the God of need and
presence showed up. Having hit my lowest place, I prayed to Jesus to help
me and Jesus said yes, and a partnership was formed that would eventually
lead to healing. I learned and met the God of presence, the God who stands
alongside us and metaphorically holds our hands in the midst of suffering;
the God who will use us, and anyone around us, to remind us of God's love
and presence for us. God won't do the work, but God will supervise. Vickie
and I learned, in our own way that we had never been alone; neither had

Nicholas. Nor had our other children, Hannah and Zachary. Co-creators with God in all of creation; not just the good stuff!

And now enters Elijah and silence. God has drawn me to silence. After traveling down all the paths of "why" and entertaining all the representatives of God held by friends and family and me alike, back to silence. Silence is trust; silence is admitting the limitations of human understanding. Life consists of so much mystery that sitting in the silence constitutes the deepest and most profound response, as does sitting quietly in sorrow and suffering. God lives in the silence. Now, even as memories of that terrible loss and others since then threaten to overwhelm, I go sit in silence and quiet all the noise so once again I can sense the presence and compassion of God right in the midst of suffering and joy.

Chapter 14

Hope, Despair, and Joy

> And this, of course, is my hope for today's sermon—that it will
> open the way for you to deal creatively with grief, and in making
> the best of it, let it in turn make the best of you.[1]

REMEMBER, I MENTIONED AN orange chair earlier. Well, a cataclysmic event took place in our home on September 9, 2020. The orange chair that I'd been sitting in for prayer and meditation for more than thirty-one years was replaced. The chair was worn out. The wood slats in the seating part were exposed as was the corner on each arm. I needed a pillow behind my back for the rear support to be of any help, and the lever to raise and lower the footrest had a personality all its own. The color had faded, dust was everywhere on the arm rests. One good slap and dust floated. And for some beautiful reason the time had come to change.

Now, lest you think this is just about a chair, let's move a bit deeper. Vickie and I inherited this chair when my parents moved to Florida. There were two chairs. The other one disappeared decades ago. This one stayed. After returning from a raucous trip to Mackinac Island in the summer of 1989, hungover and walking like I was ninety with severe back issues, life was rapidly becoming overwhelming. Nicholas had been dead a bit over six months and I tried continuously to move this grieving process forward more quickly, to circumvent as much pain as possible. Vickie and I circled back to the University of Iowa Hospital and Clinics in hopes of increasing the pace of grief. I thought that if I could only revisit the places where all the painful experiences took place, then perhaps I could accelerate the pace

1. Claypool, *Tracks*, 103.

of grieving and move these memories into the background of my mind. At the end of the trip, an insightful nurse from the clinic said, "Go home, Al. Put away the videos and pictures. Stay home. No matter what you do you cannot move through the pain of this loss any faster than time offers. Go home. Put all that away. Sit."

I went home angry and in tears. The pain presented like aftershock after aftershock after aftershock. I couldn't handle the loss and I needed help. One day I sat in the orange chair, crossed my legs, and prayed, "Jesus, I need your help. I cannot handle the pain and loss and I need help. Jesus, I turn my life with all this grief over to you and now I'll wait." From that day forward until the morning of September 9, God and I spent time together in that chair every day. At first thirty minutes for prayer, Scripture, praying for others. Then sixty minutes for prayer, Scripture, saints' lives, praying for others, meditation—a rich eleventh step in AA. There was and is no better way to begin each day than with God in Jesus, with myself, and with daily hope.

Why change now? Great question. On one level the orange chair supported a growing soul, and the new chair supports an aging body, seriously. On one level the orange chair represented God in my life; I've found that I can pray and meditate anywhere and while I enjoy "home" the most, my "home" in God's heart and God in my heart moves with me everywhere. Finally, though, the chair was falling apart.

I'm grateful for that orange chair. I took a piece of fabric and framed it and placed it on the wall in my office. And I'm grateful beyond words to God for the healing that God has brought my way since September of 1989. How did this come about?

Hope had a tough road to travel within my spirit. While hope struggled to be born within, despair retained the power to thwart. I was like a gardener trying frantically to stop the tulips and daffodils in the spring. The gardener can suppress the annual breaking forth in her or his space, but she or he cannot suppress signs of hope in the yards of neighbors, in parks, in the wild. Hope (spring) pushes away all forces of suppression and breaks forth invited or not, and comes to expression. It takes a good deal of effort to suppress hope, especially when despair becomes a new friend releasing one from the struggle to discover life again.

One level of despair showed up in mild to severe anxiety. I moved in and out of this level early after Nicholas died. Numbness held me in place for several months. The anxiety at this level reflected the fact that I had no idea of the roadmap to follow such a loss; I didn't know what I didn't know. When I realized that Nicholas was gone forever in the flesh, a deeper level of despair appeared. On this level of moderate despair, I moved from anxiety to fear. Anxiety was reflected in the fight-or-flight from grief; fear gripped me as the near conviction that I'd never be able to move on.

Fear presented many ways. Naturally there was fear for our surviving children, Hannah and Zachary. (I'm grateful to say that up until they were each eighteen, I only asked for one blood test each out of my own fear. Our pediatrician understood the fear and worked patiently with Vickie and me.) I was also afraid that I'd never heal. Since I had only theoretical understanding of healing from grief, measuring healing against that criteria increased fear as my experience didn't line up with cultural and known psychological and neurological expectations about grief. Not at all. I was afraid I'd get stuck in that incredible pain for the rest of my life. At this point, life became dangerous.

I never seriously contemplated taking my own life. The key word here is *seriously*. There is a level of despair that appeared as storm clouds on the horizon, threatening to envelop my spirit in such a level of despair that my principal options would become deep depression, alcoholism, suicide, an affair, quit the church, or try to run away from this life. What happened?

A community of angels had slowly surrounded Vickie and me during those first few years. They brought hope. Some surrounded us individually, some surrounded us together. Remember that one vulnerability of marriage after the death of a child is the unrealistic expectation that our spouse can handle our grief and their grief. There are times when each needs his or her own circle of angels.

St. Stephen's Episcopal Church is located in Fairview, Pennsylvania. It is a small congregation with about eighty people in worship on Sunday, and they have created an incredible community. I had the joy of serving as their vicar for two years. I remember thinking that if Vickie and I had a community like this to go to we would have been held lovingly in our loss for as long as necessary and without judgment. This has always been simply their gift.

Kate sat in the back pew and was known for her healing hugs. Vivian appeared as a crotchety old woman but in fact had a delightful soul and an active commitment to her church and the people. She was always, always the first person to arrive on Sunday morning. Bob sat in the back with his wife, Mary. I soon learned that they had lost two children, one as a child and the other as an adult. Their child was killed by a car that ran off the road into their front yard. Their older son died in a small airplane crash forty years later. I wanted to meet them and learn their story, so we got together.

Over coffee in their home of fifty years, surrounded by all the pictures and items of memory, they began to tell the story. Their farm sat on the major highway dividing Fairview into north and south. One day when their son George was twelve years old, he was playing in the yard when his dad noticed a car losing control and running off the road. Before he could even shout, the car had careened into their front yard, hitting and killing their son, right there. Forty years later their son Michael and his girlfriend were piloting a private plane when the engine malfunctioned and they plunged to their deaths.

I asked Bob, "How did you ever survive these losses?" He said, "The community of St. Stephen's. That's how we survived. They came over right away back when George died and began to wrap their arms around us in countless ways. We were stunned and numb and that wonderful group of people stayed by our sides through the entire experience." Bob slowly began to weep. "And the love, they loved us . . . I can't tell you how much they loved us. When we returned to church all the people wrapped themselves around us as we worshipped God and received communion. But honestly, Father, the community of people brought us back to life."

Again and again I come back to the relationship between community and hope. If the local church is the hope of the world, then hope manifests in community. Looking back, community also brought hope to my life. The community that surrounded me included my dearest and best friend Bob Myers, Hal and Linda Toberman, Dr. Ron Lee, Fr. Roy Hendricks, and my TUG (The Uncovering Group) cadre of Mike, Clarence, Jay, Nancy, Larry, and Jan. Then there were Compassionate Friends, especially Foster Roser, Bill and Jane Kindorf, Martin Smith, Michael Sparough, Cotton Fite, as well as the people of the Church of the Incarnation, the people of St. Michael's Church, Kristine, Brian, Mark, Lisa, Paul, Bernadette, Hannah, Ben, Katy and Zachary, our Mackinac Island Friends, whatever amount of empathy we had at the time between Vickie and me, and Jesus. They saw what I could not—that my life was sinking into this deepest level of despair and that borrowed hope was the only hope available. They gave and gave and gave again.

I was raised in a "pick yourself up by your bootstraps" family. (Yes, we were blessed to have boots.) With this family value as a measure of success, life became interesting when I realized that rising out of despair required, if not demanded, others helping with the bootstraps. I'm not sure I could even bend over to grasp the straps.

Over time, mystery became community, and I knew I wasn't alone. For several months it seemed that every person I met in Barrington had lost a child at various ages and for various reasons. While our story was unique in many ways, our experience was shared across age, gender, race, and creedal lines. I was not alone. Each person I met who was years from the death of their child invited hope. Others, however, clearly anesthetized their pain with anger, blame, alcohol, affairs, rigid religion, lawsuits, suicide, or drugs. I understood every path chosen. All paths remained open. Hope was not a given by any stretch of the imagination.

Where does one go when empty? With a semblance of life, we seek out others who possess what our heart craves. In this case, hope. My sister Lisa sent me an article about "balcony people" who stand "above" us or "ahead" of us on the journey of hope and have so much hope they are able to reach down and grab us by the hand and lead us into unknown places of hope. Only then did I see how blind I had become with despair; how blind I had become to the pathways out of the valley; how blind to the continued fact that I needed God and other people or my life would be a continual wandering in the valley of deep despair.

Remember the parable of the door? What happened over time was that I began to wonder how people moved forward into their lives. And when the time came that I witnessed people on the road of healing, I looked at them and remembered the occasional restaurant experience where I look at another table's food and when asked my order say repeatedly, "I'll have whatever they have." When I'm hungry I want to eat. When I'm lonely I want company. When I'm spent or blind on hope I want hopeful people and I want the clarity of sight, free from resentments, anger, blame, booze and all, so I can see with clear eyes and a loving heart what they have to offer. And eventually I wanted to join with others who experienced such a dreadful loss and become hope for them, become arms of God if you will. I wanted to become one of them.

The richest and deepest hope became a willingness to spend time with other bereaved parents and in so doing exchanging hope. Still to this day when I meet a newly bereaved parent my heart breaks, painfully aware of what is in store for them. I want to do all that I can to help them to look away from the door patiently, faithfully, and lovingly. That which we desire we receive by giving away.

It took years for me to realize the difference between joy and hope and happiness. There is a place to reach that lives beyond hope and happiness because, honestly, we cannot rely on either hope or happiness. Hope is transient and moves around with surface circumstances; happiness even moreso. Hope is meant to move us to help make the world a better place, which for me includes making the world a better place for bereaved parents. Helping certainly brings meaning, but walking with someone out of despair? Well, that becomes joy. Joy settles deeper in the human psyche and spirit. Joy is like a river that flows from a deeper river in our soul, complete with suffering, sorrow, and despair. They're all in the river of life. But in that river joy is like a deep current that flows in and through our soul moving us to helping others; helping us move our wounds to joy.

Her name is Erin. Her parents knew she would only live for about two months after she was born but she was born anyway. We celebrated her birth and her baptism. Then she died. The funeral was held at St. Michael's in front of an overflowing church out of love for Dave and Melissa. Sitting in the middle of the nave was a small white casket containing dear Erin. Somehow we made our way through the service. As we were leaving to music, Dave picked up the little casket and carried Erin out of the church. The tears erupted in all corners, from men and women alike. Dave became hope for all of us without even knowing it. He carried the burdens of his sorrow, having been presented to God, carried them out of that space and into the light and also carried out his hope and the hope of an entire congregation. Ask people today, nearly twenty years later, and everyone there will remember that one scene etched into our souls, a scene of hope.

Chapter 15

Grief Set Free

Unbind him, and let him go.[1]

THEN ONE DAY WE pass a group of bereaved parents on the same path talking and all of a sudden one begins to laugh, a deep and resounding, soulful, releasing laugh. We're startled: how does one laugh again after so great a sorrow? We become rabidly curious because we are catching glimpses of a possibility for a healed life that was invisible to us years ago but now is beginning to show up in focus. I stop and stare.

The laughter came from the face of a person where grief was naked and yet they were also alive. They continued to tell their story, as we all do, but their story was interwoven with gratitude, love, forgiveness, and grace. Tears are unapologetic as is grief; there is no closure, but with the help of others and God the burden becomes lighter, the valley is filled in, and the rough places are made plain.

Doors are visible everywhere and our mission is to keep walking, because someone is always looking for hope to change, like you and me, in a way that deeply integrates our losses and the memories of our children; free to carry our child's desire or loved one's desire for life into our lives; free to believe whatever we wish about God and grief; free to accept sorrow and suffering as integral parts of human existence; free to let go of trying to make the world into something it is not; free to see the beauty of all creation, including death and life; free from the expectations of some norm of grieving; free to laugh, dance, cry, and sing from a profound experience of the depth of human life and love.

1. John 11:44.

Years later Brother Martin Smith would challenge me to realize a simple truth: I was connected with every bereaved parent who had come before and would be connected with every bereaved parent to come, and that we had a calling to reach out to each other in our loss, to guide and help each other along the path of healing. Further, that the grief we feel, we feel for all parents and all parents feel for us; it's a deep loss that actually invites us into the broken heart of God and the grief God shares with us. My hope is that this memoir serves as an invitation to walk this path together. By our grief we free others that they may find the path to their own liberation; their own grief set free! May it be free from religious and cultural norms; free from internal fears and despair; free to sit in our sorrow and glad memories both. And may we be free to love those we see no longer in the way we wish to love them. Grief set free!

My niece Elizabeth, who herself is now on eagle's wings and alive with God, sang a favorite at Nick's memorial service, "On Eagle's Wings." Up until that day I had never heard the hymn. She had a beautiful voice, and her notes rose beyond the ceiling into the sunshine, lifting hearts and souls to God. No one sang the chorus. She offered the solo and we cried and appreciated a moment of spiritual peace before the service ended. Since then, I've probably heard or sung the song at just about every funeral I've either led or been to for thirty years. There's comfort in this hymn. In the Psalms, the writer says God will lift us up on eagle's wings. In one sense, then, we all hope the wings can carry us when that time comes, right through the ceiling, into the Son, into the light, into the heart of the Divine. The following is a fable.

> It was raining in the forest. It had been raining for days, and all the birds and animals were drenched. The eagle, too, was drenched, and his spirits dampened as well, for his mate lay with a chill, a victim of the constant rain. There was no way to keep her dry and the eagle looked on with despair as her life slowly drained away. His tears mingled with the rain when she died.
>
> It was raining in the forest. The eagle could not stand the rain. It brought back memories too painful for him to bear. He rose up from the trees, hoping in flight to escape his thoughts. Higher and higher he climbed, until finally he broke through the dark clouds into the dazzling sunlight that lay beyond. As the warm sun dried his wings, he suddenly realized that the healing sun had been there all the time his mate had needed it. The pain of knowledge learned

too late was more than he could stand, and there were tears for the sun to dry.

It was raining in the forest. It had been raining for days, and all the birds and animals were drenched. The rabbit, too, was drenched, and her spirits dampened as well, for her child lay with a chill, a victim of the constant rain. She poured out her sad tale to all who would listen, but the other creatures, too, were victims of the rain, and none could help. An eagle happened by, and the rabbit began to tell her tale to him. But she had hardly started speaking when the eagle suddenly lifted the rabbit's dying child onto his wings and began to circle quickly up into the dark and stormy clouds on an errand he did not take time to explain.[2]

Our pain and grief bring healing to us and others! Grief set free!

2. Armstrong, *Minister*, 57.

Epilogue

NICK'S ASHES ARE INTERRED in the columbarium in the chapel of St. Michael's Episcopal Church in Barrington, Illinois. Vickie and I have our niches on either side of him, fulfilling our promise to be buried with him. However, there is a little garden in memory of Nicholas on Market Street on Mackinac Island. It was created by our friends, Tony and Loretta Spata. In that garden, on that sacred island where he had the best summer of his life, a bit of Nick's ashes rest in the beauty of the flowers, the lilac trees, and the love. When Zach and Katy got married, they stopped there for prayer on the way to the wedding. A gentle quiet enfolds his garden. We're grateful.

All sorts of people ask me if I miss Nicholas. And the answer is always the same; yes, yes, and yes, to the depths of my soul. Losing him was losing a part of myself never to be recovered in this life. A room lives in my heart and the room has his name on the door. I can go to that room anytime I want and visit the entire story of his life and death. Knowing the room is there is comforting. Early after his death I lived most of my life in or near that room. Not so much now. If I sit in that room for some time, however, the suffering and sorrow and joy will move to the forefront of my life once again, bringing memory upon memory.

I'm asked if I ever think of what he might look like today? For a few years I'd try to envision what he looked like, but simply wasn't able to do so. They ask, don't you wonder what he'd be like if he were still alive? Of course, I wonder that at times. But I refuse to let what might have been blind me to the beauty and wonder of life today: Vickie, Hannah, Ben, Zachary, Katy, countless friends and a wider family. And a present God.

Spending time wondering what he might look like today diminishes what his life actually was and suggests that his life was less than any other life. His life was certainly shorter than many other lives, but in no way less than. Nick faced the truth of his life and death with courage. He died with faith. By directly facing Nicholas's life and the pain and joy therein, I'm able to remember the fullness and completeness of his life. I don't need to spend time wondering what might have been. No, I give thanks for what was and what is now. Do I wish he was still alive today? Yes, but as Stephen King writes in his book *11/22/63*,[1] what we want is for the dead person to be alive in the life we have now and with no changes. Take a forty-year-old Nicholas and drop him right into this life today? King's book gives an excellent portrayal of what happens when wishes of past lives are fulfilled in the present. Life moves forward. We can move backwards but life moves forward and the challenge for all us bereaved parents is to get back in the river of life and bring our human experience with us. And if all of a sudden a forty-year-old Nicholas drops into this life, then the gifts and legacy of Nicholas are lost.

Nicholas left many gifts. He taught me the value of having and cherishing children. He helped me shift my personal values to put family and God above the church, such that I made every one of Hannah's and Zach's activities growing up and visited them often while they were in college. The experience strengthened Vickie's and my marriage and drew new friends into our lives. And Nicholas made me a better priest. Like all bereaved parents, I wish I could learn these lessons in a different way but that's not how life works.

Nicholas was named after the youngest son in the TV series *Eight Is Enough*. Most think he's named after the saint. Not so. He and I celebrated many things together in his short life. We shared a beer. He drove our car often. We shared a cigar. And then one day the time came when nothing more would be added to his life; no more shopping, no more games, no more restaurants, no more anything. Just him and his beautiful, wonderful, inspiring life. After life, death, sorrow, suffering, hope, happiness, and joy comes gratitude, giving thanks for all of life and specifically for Nicholas. Giving thanks reminds me that his life was never mine to possess. Nicholas was and is a gift that was my joy to help love for his life. Words cannot grasp my deep love and gratitude for him and the anticipation of "seeing" him again in the great beyond, both of us unbound and set free!

---

1. King, *11/22/63*, jacket.

Bibliography

Alcoholics Anonymous. *The Big Book*. New York: Alcoholics Anonymous, 1939.

The Book of Common Prayer. New York: Church, 1979.

Alison, James. *Faith Beyond Resentment: Fragments Catholic and Gay*. New York: Crossroad, 2001.

Armstrong, William. *Minister, Heal Thyself*. New York: Pilgrim, 1985.

Becker, Ernest. *The Denial of Death*. New York: Free, 1973.

Christensen, Carl Waldo. *Waves on the Sand*. Wilmette, IL: Fox, 1991.

Claypool, John. *Tracks of a Fellow Struggler: How to Handle Grief*. Waco, TX: Word, 1974.

The Compassionate Friends. 2016. *Marriage Study*. www.compassionatefriends.org.

Flint, Annie Johnson. *He Giveth More Grace*. Plymouth, MA: Hayden, 2019.

Friedman, Edwin H. *Generation to Generation: Family Process in Church and Synagogue*. New York: Guilford, 1985.

Frost, Robert. *Mountain Interval*. New York: Holt, 1916.

Herman, Judith Lewis. *Trauma and Recovery: The Aftermath of Violence—From Domestic Abuse to Political Terror*. New York: Basic, 1992.

King, Stephen. *11/22/63*. New York: Scribner, 2016.

Kubler-Ross, Elisabeth. *On Death and Dying: What the Dying have to Teach Doctors, Nurses, Clergy, and Their Own Family*. New York: Scribner, 1969.

Lewis, Randy. *No Greatness Without Goodness: How a Father's Love Changed a Company and Sparked a Movement*. Carol Stream, IL: Tyndale, 2014.

Nouwen, Henri J. M. *The Inner Voice of Love: A Journey Through Anguish to Freedom*. New York: Doubleday, 1998.

Nye, Naomi Shihab. *Everything Comes Next: Collected and New Poems*. New York: Greenwillow, 2020.

Osgood, Judy, ed. *Meditations for Bereaved Parents*. Sunriver, OR: Gilgal, 1983.

Primack, Joel R., and Nancy Ellen Abrams. *The View from the Center of the Universe: Discovering Our Extraordinary Place in the Cosmos*. New York: Riverhead, 2006.

Rohr, Richard. *Falling Upward: A Spirituality for the Two Halves of Life*. San Francisco: Jossey-Bass, 2011.

Schiff, Harriet Sarnoff. *The Bereaved Parent*. Middlesex: Penguin, 1977.

Wells, Samuel. *A Future That's Bigger Than the Past: Catalysing Kingdom Communities*. Norwich: Canterbury, 2019.

Wolterstorff, Nicholas. *Lament for a Son*. Grand Rapids: Eerdmans, 1987.

Made in the USA
Coppell, TX
06 February 2022